TABLE OF CON

Introduction - Memories	3
Measurement Conversions	4
Important Notes	5
Story Tellers	6
Momma's Words	7
Desserts	
Pies	8-19
Social Affairs	20
Pie Crusts	21-22
Grandmommy and Granddaddy	23
Cookies	25-32
The Airplane	33
Cakes	34-48
The Trip to Washington	49
Candy	51-54
Granny and Pop-Pa	55
How to Keep a Husband	56
Icing	57-59
Misc Desserts	60-64
The Trip to Washington	65
Panther Almost got that Woman	66
Side Dishes	67-76
Shot that was Directed by a Bible Verse	77
Main Dishes	78
Breakfast	79-81
Beef Dishes	82-83
Tex Mex	84-88
Chicken Dishes	89-90
Fish Dishes	91
Seafood Dishes	92-93
Pork Dishes	95-95
Wild Meat Dishes	96-97
Bimbo	98
My Favorite Memories and Recipes	99
Breads	100-104
My Favorite Memories and Recipes	105
Sundays at Grandmommys House	106

MEMORIES

I had not really looked at all of Granny's, Momma's, Grandmommy's, cookbooks. What I found was absolutely priceless. There were recipes written on pieces of paper, on envelopes, scratch pads, etc. After looking through all of their 'handwritten' notes for their recipes and also notes that were written to them on other recipes I decided that I needed to preserve these memories in a cookbook. They would want their 'girls' to have the recipes to share with their families and then keep passing these recipes down through all of our families and friends.

It was such fun remembering things they would say when they were cooking. Remembering things they would do is hilarious. The superstitions and old Wives' Tales that would be carried out are priceless. Even though these recipes are from all kinds of cookbooks, and more from other family members, they made them 'their' recipes when they would make them with just a 'dash' of something different.

Some very easy recipes, some not-so-complicated recipes, and some complicated recipes from past years. The notes are written to our loved ones who have such great memories that need to be shared.

Our families were "old school", raised on farms and ranches where the meal was meant to provide you with the nourishment needed to get you from breakfast to lunch to dinner. All cooks add a touch that is "their touch alone" to recipes that no one else can do or would think to add. So take these recipes and make them 'your own' remembering your Momma, Granny, Grandmommy as you cook. They will be smiling down from heaven, happy you have left some great memories to and with your family.

Blessings,
Linda Howard

Measurement Conversions

1 Gallon Equals:
Four (4) Quarts
Eight (8) Pints
Sixteen (16) Cups
Twenty-Eight (28) Ounces
3.8 Liters

One (1) Quart
Two (2) Pints
Four (4) Cups
Thirty-Two (32) Ounces
.95 Liters

One (1) Pint
Two (2) Cups
Sixteen (16) Ounces
473 ML

One (1) Cup
Sixteen (16) Tablespoons
Eight (8) Ounces
240 ML

1/2 Cup
Eight (8) Tablespoons
Four (4) Ounces
120 ML

1/4 Cup
Four (4) Tablespoons
Two (2) Ounces
60 ML

One (1) Tablespoon
Three (3) Teaspoons
1/2 Ounces
15 ML

One (1) Teaspoon
Five (5) ML

Important Notes

1. ## Oleo equals Margarine

   You can substitute butter, or various oils (think coconut, olive, and avacado) for oleo measure for measure

2. ## Scant means 'just barely'

   If a recipe calls for a scant tablespoon then you would do a tablespoon that is loosely measured, not packed or heaped.

3. ## Cooking Times Vary

   Depending on where you live, the type of oven you use will affect the cooking time of a dish. Always check on dishes throughout the cooking time to ensure they are not under or over cooked. Always cook items throughly.

4. ## Refrigeration | Freezing Times Vary

   As above refridgerators and freezers may vary. Always plan ahead if yours takes longer.

5. ## Duplicates

   You will find multiple duplicate recipe names within these pages. Each of these recipes, just as explained in the introduction, was different and came from mothers and grandmothers. Take them and make them your own.

Story Tellers

Throughout this recipe book, you will find stories
told by Know Scott, my grandfather.
Not only did he tell these stories, the stories were published in the Paris News.
Families from all walks of life were intertwined during those days.

From the 1916 Paris Fire to the building of Pat Mayse my family had the privilege to know many people who made a lastly impact on the Red River Valley. The stories I share, I share as a promise to my Momma, who loved to write, and as a testimony to a way of life long since gone. Maybe they will inspire you to tell some tales of your own just as you write new recipes include new stories both fiction and non-fiction.

MOMMA'S WORDS

When my sweet Momma went to Heaven at the age of 94, she left behind all kinds of treasures for us to find. I never knew that she wrote poetry, but we found little poems written on scraps of paper hidden in all sorts of places that she knew we would find when packing up all of her life.
These that we found I have kept close to my heart.

DEAR LORD

Dear Lord, I am 80 and there is so much I haven't done,
I hope Dear Lord, you will let me live until I'm 81,
But if I haven't finished what I want to do,
Would you please let me stay awhile until I'm 82?
So many places I want to go, so much I want to see -
Do you think you could manage to make it 83?
Many things I may have done, But there's so much left in store,
I'll like it very much, to live to 84.
And if by then, I'm still alive, then I'd like to stay to 85.
The world is changing very fast, so I'd really like to stick around
and see what happens to the world when I am 86.
I know, Dear Lord it is a lot to ask, and it will be nice in Heaven;
But I'd really like to stay around until I'm 87.
I know by then I won't be fast, and sometimes I'll be late,
But it would be oh_so_pleasant to be around at 88!
I have seen so many things and had a wonderful time
I'm sure that I'll be willing to leave at 89.
Maybe!

THOUGHTS

When thoughts don't come as easily
As once they did to me,
To think that I am getting old
Is pure absurdity.
It's true there is snow upon my roof
My steps a bit confused,
But I'm not getting old, you see
I'm just a little used!

Desserts First? Yes, Please!

Always lovingly made and always plentiful for any special occasions even if that was Sunday dinner after Church.

PIES

A place to write new recipes or create your own.

PEANUT BUTTER PIE

INGREDIENTS
- 3 Eggs
- 1 cup dark corn syrup
- ½ cup sugar
- 1 teaspoon vanilla
- ½ cup creamy peanut butter

DIRECTIONS
- Mix all ingredients and pour into an unbaked pie shell.
- Bake at 350 degrees for 30 minutes.

ICEBOX PIE

INGREDIENTS
- 1 large can evaporated milk (chilled and whipped)
- 1 cup sugar
- 1 pkg each Jello (raspberry and strawberry)
- 1 cup hot water
- 1 box Vanilla Wafers
- 1 cup fruit (Bananas, Cherries, or Pineapple)

DIRECTIONS
- Dissolve Jello in 1 cup of hot water.
- Mix with milk.
- Line pan with vanilla wafers and then add fruit.
- Pour mixture over wafers and fruit.
- Set in icebox for 2 hours.

LEMON PIE

INGREDIENTS
- 1 can condensed milk
- 2 egg yolks
- ½ cup lemon juice
- 1 cooked pie shell

DIRECTIONS
- Mix together and cook over medium heat until done, about 5 minutes
- Pour into cooked pie shell
- Put in refrigerator until set up

PINK LEMONADE PIE

INGREDIENTS
- 1 cup 3-minute brand oats
- 3 tablespoons Brown Sugar
- $\frac{1}{3}$ cup Walnuts, chopped
- $\frac{1}{3}$ cup melted Butter
- 1 (16 oz) can of Pink Lemonade, thawed
- 1 (15 oz) can sweetened condensed Milk
- 1 (9 oz) container frozen dessert topping

DIRECTIONS
- Spread oats on a baking sheet.
- Bake at 350 degrees for 10 minutes.
- Toss with sugar, nuts, and butter.
- Press evenly on the bottom and sides of the 9-inch pie plate.
- Refrigerate.
- Combine lemonade and milk.
- Fold in dessert topping and pour into chilled oatmeal crust.
- Refrigerate at least 4 hours before serving.

PINEAPPLE PIE

INGREDIENTS
- 3 egg yolks
- 3 tablespoons of sugar
- 1 tablespoon melted butter (unsalted)
- 4 tablespoons flour
- Pinch of salt
- 1 and ½ cups milk
- 1 cup sugar
- 1 small can of crushed pineapple
- 1 baked pie shell

DIRECTIONS
- Beat egg yolks
- Add melted butter and ¾ cup milk.
- Mix flour and sugar together.
- Add flour and sugar mixture to egg mixture and add pineapple and the rest of the milk
- Cook in a double boiler until thick
- Pour into baked pie shells
- Beat egg whites with 1 tablespoon sugar for each egg
- Put on top of the pie and bake at 350 degrees until the top is browned.

Notes

CHEESECAKE PIE

Preparing 30 Minutes
Cooking 55 Minutes
Serve 4 hours

INGREDIENTS

CRUMB CRUST:
- 2 cups fine Vanilla Wafer or
- Graham Cracker crumbs
- 6 tablespoons butter or margarine, melted
- ¼ cup sugar

FILLING:
- 12 oz cream cheese, softened
- ⅔ cup sugar
- 3 eggs
- 2 tablespoons lemon juice
- 1 (11 oz) can of Campbell's condensed
- Cheddar Cheese soup, undiluted
- 1 teaspoon grated lemon rind
- 1 teaspoon Vanilla Extract
- ¼ teaspoon Almond Extract

TOPPING:
- 1 cup sour cream
- ¼ cup Sugar
- 1 teaspoon grated lemon rind
- 1 teaspoon Vanilla Extract

DIRECTIONS

TO MAKE CRUST:
- Combine crumbs, butter, and sugar.
- Press firmly into a 10-inch pie shell.
- Chill for 1 hour

CHEESECAKE PIE CONT'D

Preparing  **Cooking** **Serve**
30 Minutes   55 Minutes   4 hours

DIRECTIONS

TO MAKE FILLING:
- In a mixing bowl blend cream cheese until smooth.
- Blend sugar and eggs alternately into cream cheese on medium speed.
- Blend in 1 cup of Campbell's soup, lemon juice, lemon rind, and flavorings.
- Pour into chilled pie crust.
- Bake at 350 degrees for 50 minutes

MEANWHILE – FOR TOPPING...
- Blend sour cream, remaining soup, sugar, lemon rind, and vanilla.
- Spread on pie.
- Bake 5 minutes more. Cool, chill
- Garnish chilled cheesecake with cherry pie filling.

   ***Granny says you can make 2 smaller pie shells
      If so cook each for 30 to 35 minutes.***

PECAN PIE

INGREDIENTS

- 1 cup sugar
- 1 cup corn syrup
- 2 tablespoons Butter
- 1 teaspoon Vanilla
- 1 tablespoon flour
- 2 eggs
- 1 cup pecans
- 1 unbaked pie crust

DIRECTIONS

- Mix well all ingredients except pecans and pour into an unbaked pie shell
- Lay pecans on top and bake very slowly at 200 degrees for 30 minutes
- Check to see if thick – if not bake it for 30 more minutes until thick

BUTTER PECAN PIE

INGREDIENTS

- $\frac{1}{8}$ lb butter (unsalted)
- ½ cup sugar
- ¼ teaspoon salt
- 1 cup dark corn syrup
- 3 eggs
- 1 cup pecan halves
- 1 unbaked pie crust

DIRECTIONS

- Stir the butter to soften and add sugar slowly
- beating the mixture until fluffy.
- Add salt and syrup and beat well.
- Add eggs one at a time beating thoroughly
- after each egg.
- Stir in pecans and pour into unbaked pie crust.
- Bake at 350 degrees for at least 45 minutes.
- Cool for 3 hours

FRENCH COCONUT PIE

INGREDIENTS

- 1 stick oleo
- 1 ½ cups sugar
- 3 whole eggs
- 1 tablespoon vinegar
- 1 teaspoon vanilla extract
- 1 can Angel Flake Coconut
- 1 unbaked pie crust

DIRECTIONS

- Combine all ingredients and pour into an unbaked pie shell.
- Bake in a moderate oven at 350 degrees for 1 hour.

PINEAPPLE CHESS PIE

INGREDIENTS

- 1 and ½ cups sugar
- 3 very scant tablespoons flour
- 1 stick oleo
- 3 eggs
- 1 small can of crushed pineapple, drained
- 1 unbaked pie shell

DIRECTIONS

- Mix in order.
- Bake in an unbaked pie shell for 45 minutes on 375 degrees

SOUTHERN PECAN PIE

INGREDIENTS

- 1 cup Sugar
- ½ cup Corn Syrup
- ¼ cup Oleo
- 3 Eggs (well beaten)
- 1 cup Pecans

DIRECTIONS

- Mix all ingredients and pour into unbaked pie crust.
- Bake at 375 degrees for 40 minutes or until mixture is solid.

BUTTERMILK PIE

INGREDIENTS
- 1 stick Butter
- 2 cups Sugar
- 3 tablespoons Flour
- 3 Eggs
- 1 cup Buttermilk

DIRECTIONS
- Mix all ingredients until smooth.
- Place in an unbaked pie crust and cook at 350 degrees for 45 minutes.

KISS PIE

INGREDIENTS
- 3 egg whites
- 1 cup sugar
- 1 teaspoon vanilla extract
- 10 soda crackers
- 1 cup nuts

DIRECTIONS
- Beat egg whites until stiff.
- Fold in sugar and slowly add vanilla.
- Crush soda crackers and fold them into a mixture.
- Pour into a greased and floured pie pan.
- Bake at 350 degrees for 20 to 25 minutes.

RAISIN PIE

INGREDIENTS
- 1 cup sugar
- 1 stick butter, softened
- 1 tablespoon flour
- 1 teaspoon cinnamon
- 1 egg
- 1 cup raisins (cooked and drained)
- 1 unbaked pie shell

DIRECTIONS
- Mix all ingredients together and pour into an unbaked pie shell.
- Bake at 350 degrees for 40 to 45 minutes or until the mixture is thick.

CREAMY PUMPKIN PIE

INGREDIENTS
- 1 box Dream Whip
- cup milk
- 1 pkg instant Vanilla Pudding
- ¼ teaspoon cinnamon
- 1 cup pumpkin
- ¼ teaspoon nutmeg
- ¼ cup ginger
- 1 cooked pie shell

DIRECTIONS
- Prepare Dream Whip and add pumpkin.
- Add milk, pudding, and spices.
- Refrigerate until set.

ANOTHER LEMON PIE

INGREDIENTS
CRUMB CRUST:
- 8 Graham Crackers, mashed
- ½ stick unsalted butter, melted
- ½ cup brown sugar, packed

FILLING:
- 1 can Eagle Brand Milk
- 3 lemons (squeezed)
- 3 egg yolks
- Whipped Cream

DIRECTIONS
CRUMB CRUST:
- Mix all of the ingredients together for a crust
- Press into pie pans and shape

FILLING:
- Mix together and cook over medium heat until done, about 5 minutes
- Pour into graham cracker crust
- Chill and then put whipped cream on top

BANANA CREAM PIE

INGREDIENTS

- 2 egg yolks, slightly beaten
- 1 ¾ cups milk
- 1 regular size Vanilla Pudding
- and Pie Filling Mix
- 2 bananas
- 2 egg whites
- ¼ teaspoon Cream of Tarter
- ¼ cup sugar
- 1 baked pie shell

DIRECTIONS

- Mix egg yolks, milk, and pudding in a 2 qt saucepan.
- Cook and stir over medium heat until the mixture bubbles (about 5 minutes).
- Cool
- Slice bananas into baked pie shell.
- Spread filling over bananas.
- Beat egg whites until foamy and then add cream of tartar and sugar.
- Beat until forms a peak.
- Put on top of the pie and bake at 350 degrees for 12 to 15 minutes.

SWEET POTATO PIE

INGREDIENTS

- 3 cups sweet potatoes
- 2 and ½ cups sugar
- 4 eggs
- ½ lb butter
- 1 teaspoon cinnamon
- 1 teaspoon cloves
- 2 teaspoons vanilla
- 1 can of evaporated milk
- 1 uncooked pie shell

DIRECTIONS

- Cook potatoes and mash.
- Mix sugar, eggs, and spices.
- Soften butter and mix with potatoes.
- Add sugar mixture to potatoes and butter.
- Mix well.
- Add milk and stir until smooth.
- Pour into uncooked pie shell.
- Bake at 350 degrees for 45 minutes or until the knife placed in the center of the pie comes out clean.

ANOTHER COCONUT PIE

INGREDIENTS

- 1 ¾ cup Sugar
- 4 Eggs
- ½ cup Flour
- ½ cup Oleo
- 2 cups Milk
- 1 ½ cups Coconut
- 1 teaspoon Vanilla

DIRECTIONS

- Mix all ingredients together and pour into a 10-inch pie pan.
- Bake at 350 degrees for 45 minutes.
- This pie makes its own crust.

CHOCOLATE PIE

INGREDIENTS

- 3 cups Sugar
- ½ cup Cocoa
- ½ cup Flour
- 3 Egg Yolks (beaten)
- 3 ½ cups Milk (use 1 can evaporated milk and 1 can water)
- ¼ lb. Oleo

DIRECTIONS

- Cook in double boiler until smooth and creamy.
- Make sure thick not runny.
- Pour into baked pie crust.
- Fix egg whites – beat until fluffy then add 1 tablespoon sugar
- per egg white. Beat until itands at a peak.
- Put pie and brown in oven at 350 degrees.

Yet Another Coconut Pie

INGREDIENTS

- 2 cups Sugar
- 4 tablespoons Flour
- 2 cups Milk
- 6 Egg Yolks
- 1 stick Butter
- 1 teaspoon Vanilla
- Cook until creamy and thick.

DIRECTIONS

- Cook until creamy and thick.
- Add butter and vanilla. Stir until melted.
- Add coconut until thick (will not drop off a spoon).
- Beat egg whites until fluffy – add 1 tablespoon sugar for each egg white and continue beating until forms a peek.
- Put egg whites on the pie and bake at 350 degrees until egg whites are brown.

Pineapple-Coconut Pie

INGREDIENTS

- 2 cups Sugar
- 3 Eggs
- 2 teaspoons Flour
- 2 teaspoons Corn Meal
- 1 teaspoon Vanilla
- Pinch of Salt
- 1 stick Butter
- 1 small can crushed Pineapple
- ½ cup Coconut

DIRECTIONS

- Mix all ingredients as listed
- Pour into an uncooked pie shell.
- Bake in slow oven 325 degrees for 30 to 35 minutes or until knife placed in center of pie comes out clean

Another Chocolate Pie

INGREDIENTS

- 2 cups Sugar
- 2 cups Milk
- 4 tablespoons Flour
- 4 tablespoons Cocoa
- 6 Egg Yolks
- 1 stick Butter
- 1 teaspoon Vanilla

DIRECTIONS

- Cook over a double boiler until smooth, thick, and creamy.
- Pour into baked pie crust.
- Fix egg whites – beat until fluffy then add 1 tablespoon sugar for each egg yolk and beat until comes to a peak.
- Put on the pie and bake at 350 degrees until egg whites are brown.

Coconut Pie

INGREDIENTS

- 4 eggs
- 1 ¾ cup Sugar
- ½ cup Flour
- ½ cup Oleo
- 2 cups Milk
- 1 ½ cups Coconut
- 1 teaspoon Vanilla

DIRECTIONS

- Combine all ingredients and mix well.
- Pour into a 10-inch pie pan (greased).
- Bake at 350 degrees for 45 minutes.
- This pie makes its own crust.

PEPPERMINT STICK CHIFFON PIE

Preparing
15 Minutes

 **Cooking**
5 Minutes

 Serve
2 hours

INGREDIENTS

- 1 envelope of unflavored gelatin
- ½ cup cold water
- ¼ teaspoon peppermint flavoring
- 3 egg whites
- ⅓ cup sugar
- 1 cup whipping cream, whipped
- ½ cup of crushed peppermint candy
- 2 tablespoons crushed peppermint candy
- 1 baked pie crust

DIRECTIONS

- Have a baked pie crust ready.
- Soften gelatin in water in a quart saucepan.
- Cook stirring constantly over medium heat until the mixture bubbles and the gelatin is dissolved.
- Take from heat.
- Cool and stir in peppermint flavoring.
- Beat egg whites in a bowl until foamy.
- Beat in sugar with egg whites gradually until glossy.
- Beat in gelatin mixture into the egg white/sugar mixture at low speed.
- Fold in whipped cream and ½ cup candy.
- Heap in pie shell.
- Chill for 2 hours.
- Sprinkle 2 tablespoons candy on top of the pie before serving.

LEMON MERINGUE PIE

INGREDIENTS

- ½ cup lemon juice
- 1 teaspoon grated lemon rind
- 1 1/3 cup Eagle Brand Milk
- 2 egg yolks (beaten)
- ¼ teaspoon Cream of Tarter
- 4 tablespoons sugar

DIRECTIONS

- Combine juice and rind.
- Gradually stir in Eagle Brand Milk.
- Add egg yolks and stir until well blended.
- Cook in the microwave for 2 minutes.
- Pour into a crumb crust pie shell (you can also use a regular cooked pie crust)
- Add cream of tartar to egg whites and beat until almost stiff.
- Add 1 tablespoon sugar for each egg white and beat until
  forms a peek.
- Pile onto pie and bake at 325 degrees until lightly brown – about 15 minutes.

LEMON PIE

INGREDIENTS

- 5 tablespoons Sunkist Lemon Juice
- ½ cup Water
- 1 teaspoon grated Lemon Rind
- 1 tablespoon Butter
- 1 cup Sugar
- ¼ teaspoon Salt
- 2 Egg Yolks (beaten)
- 6 tablespoons Flour
- Or 3 tablespoons Cornstarch

DIRECTIONS

- Beat sugar, salt, and flour/cornstarch together.
- Add water and cook until clear.
- Add lemon juice, grated lemon rind, and butter.
- Add beaten egg yolks and cook for 2 minutes.
- Pour into a baked pie shell.
- May make meringue out of egg whites.
- Beat until foamy and then add 1 tablespoon sugar for each egg white. Beat until forms a peek.
- Cook in oven until meringue is brown (350 degrees).

CRUSTLESS PUMPKIN PIE

INGREDIENTS

- 1-16 oz can solid pack pumpkin
- 12oz can of evaporated milk (Pet Milk)
- 2 Eggs
- ¾ cup Sugar
- 1 teaspoon Cinnamon
- ¼ teaspoon ground Allspice
- ¼ teaspoon ground Ginger
- 1/8 teaspoon Salt
- ½ cup Graham Crackers

DIRECTIONS

- Mix pumpkin, milk, and eggs together until smooth.
- Mix in sugar and spices.
- Stir in graham cracker crumbs.
- Grease a 9-inch pie pan and pour in the filling.
- Bake at 325 degrees for 45 to 55 minutes or until a knife inserted in the center comes out clean.

BAKED COCONUT CRUST

INGREDIENTS

- 2 cups Coconut
- ¼ cup melted Butter

DIRECTIONS

- Combine coconut with butter.
- Evenly press over the bottom and sides of an 8-inch pie pan.
- Bake at 300 degrees for 25 to 30 minutes or until golden brown.
- Cool

COCONUT PIE (Momma's RECIPE)

Preparing  **Cooking** **Serve**
20 Minutes 45 Minutes 1 hours

INGREDIENTS

- 1 cup Sugar
- 2 tablespoons butter
- 5 tablespoons flour
- 1 teaspoon vanilla
- 2 egg yolks
- 1 ½ cups milk
- Coconut (1 ½ cups or more if needed)

DIRECTIONS

- Mix all dry ingredients together.
- Add milk and mix well.
- Beat egg yolks and slowly add to the mixture.
- Cook over a double boiler until thick.
- Add butter and vanilla and mix until melted.
- Add coconut and pour into baked pie crust.

(Can make in the microwave- follow these instructions)

- Mix all dry ingredients and add milk.
- Put in a glass bowl and cook in microwave for 1 minute.
- Beat egg yolks add some mixture and stir well.
- Then add to the rest of the mixture.
- Cook for 2-minute intervals until thick.
- Add coconut and pour into baked pie crust.

Meringue Topping

- Beat egg whites until fluffy.
- Add 1 tablespoon Sugar for each egg white and continue to beat until forms a peek.
- Bake at 350 degrees until egg whites are brown.

CHOCOLATE PIE (Momma's RECIPE)

Preparing
20 Minutes

Cooking
45 Minutes

Serve
1 hours

INGREDIENTS

- 1 ½ cups milk
- 4 tablespoons cocoa
- 1 cup sugar
- 2 tablespoons butter
- 5 tablespoons flour
- 1 teaspoon vanilla
- 2 egg yolks
- A dash salt

DIRECTIONS

- Mix all dry ingredients and then add milk.
- Beat egg yolks and then add to the mixture.
- Cook over a double boiler until thick and creamy.
- Pour into baked pie crust.

(Can make in the microwave- follow these instructions)

- Put in a glass bowl and cook in the microwave for 1 minute.
- Beat egg yolks
- Add some mixture and stir well.
- Then add to the rest of the mixture.
- Cook for 2-minute intervals until thick.

Meringue Topping

- Beat egg whites until fluffy.
- Add 1 tablespoon Sugar for each egg white and continue to beat until forms a peek.
- Bake at 350 degrees until egg whites are brown.

SOCIAL AFFAIRS – MANY YEARS AGO

When Grandad had his 72nd birthday it took his memory back to his childhood and his mother and the stories she told him.
She had married a man named Allen who was killed in the battle at Shiloh and some years later married my great-grandfather but before that, she had come to Greenville, Texas as a child to live with her grandmother, my great-great-great-grandmother.

After her grandmother's death, she lived with the Fuller family and their daughter Sally, was her best friend. Granddad said his Mother would say that she and Sally attended many of the social affairs of that day – weddings, dances,
house raisings, and picnics. They rode horseback and as far as McKinney.
Then to Old Tarrant, the county seat of Hopkins County at the time, sometimes to Bonham and often to Cow Hill which became Commerce, and to the Jernigan's. There were 2 Jernigan families living at Cow Hill. One lived a few miles northeast near the Jernigan Thicket. The thicket covered a large part of what is now Yowell, Pecan Gap, and Jot'em Down Store and Gin.

They sometimes had to start early, even before daylight, and ride across the prairie. His mother said their riding skirts and sometimes their shoes would get wet from the dew on the grass so tall it reached nearly to the horses' shoulders. She said there was not a good riding switch to be had along the way as there was no timber except some large cottonwoods and oaks that grew along
North and South Sulphur Creeks.
His mother said she and Sally enjoyed their trips and they were always welcome whatever the occasion. They often had to spend the night when it was a wedding or a rare celebration.

Can you imagine letting your child or teenager do any of this now?

PIE CRUST

INGREDIENTS

- 2 ½ cups Flour, sifted
- 1 teaspoon Salt
- ¾ cup Shortening
- 5 tablespoons Ice Water

DIRECTIONS

- Sift flour and salt into a bowl. Add ½ of the shortening and
- cut into flour mixture with a pastry blender then add the
- other ½ shortening cutting into the flour mixture until well blended
- Do not leave any large pieces of the mixture
- Knead dough and then roll it out and place it in the pie pan
- Bake at 425 degrees for 10 to 15 minutes

FRIED PIE CRUST

INGREDIENTS

- 5 cups flour
- 3 tablespoons sugar
- 1 teaspoon baking powder
- 1 cup Crisco (solid)
- 1 teaspoon salt
- 1 large can of evaporated milk

DIRECTIONS

- Mix dry ingredients and then cut in Crisco with pastry blender
- Add milk and blend well
- Roll into small balls and roll out for pies
- Add ¼ cup of filling of your choice.
- Dampen edges of crust with water and then crink edges together
- Best when fried in an iron skillet
- Can bake in the oven until crust is brown and done (bake on 400 degrees about 10 minutes)

BAKED COCONUT CRUST

INGREDIENTS

- 2 cups coconut
- ¼ cup melted butter

DIRECTIONS

- Combine coconut with butter.
- Evenly press over the bottom and sides of an 8-inch pie pan.
- Bake at 300 degrees for 25 to 30 minutes or until golden brown.
- Cool

HOT WATER PIE CRUST

INGREDIENTS

- 1/2 cup Crisco (Soild)
- ¼ cup hot water
- 1 1/2 cups flour
- 1/2 teaspoon baking powder
- 1/4 teaspoon salt

DIRECTIONS

- CPour hot water over Crisco
- While cooling, mix flour, baking powder, and salt
- Mix and work well
- When a really cool - roll out
- Put in a pie pan and bake with any kind of filling

GrandMommy and GrandDaddy

W.A. Locke Sr. loved Hattie Brannock.

He went and purchased a surrey, and she finished her chores and met him. Then they left to be married.

Seems such a simple story and one movies are made of. Their love spanned 54 years before GrandDaddy died from a heart attack. They had six children, three girls and three boys. Which led to many grandchildren, great-grandchildren, great-great-grandchildren, and now great-great-grandchildren.

Many of my favorite memories were at my grandparent's home. I always looked forward to the time with them, my uncles, aunts, and cousins. Those of us left still tell the stories and are trying to pass them on to our children and grandchildren.

COOKIES

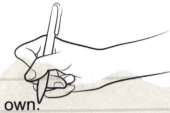

A place to write new recipes or create your own.

BOILED COOKIES

Preparing
10 Minutes

 **Cooking**
10 Minutes

 **Serve**
1 -2 hours

INGREDIENTS

- Sauce pan
- Large bowl
- 3 cups quick cooking Oatmeal
- 1 teaspoon Salt
- 4 tablespoons Cocoa
- 1 cup Coconut
- 1 cup Nuts
- 2 cups white Sugar
- ½ cup Butter
- ½ cup Milk

DIRECTIONS

MIX IN LARGE BOWL-

- 3 cups quick cooking Oatmeal
- 1 teaspoon Salt
- 4 tablespoons Cocoa
- 1 cup Coconut
- 1 cup Nuts

BRING TO A BOIL IN A SAUCEPAN -

- 2 cups white Sugar
- ½ cup Butter
- ½ cup Milk

ADD BOILING MIXTURE TO INGREDIENTS IN BOWL-

- Stir in quickly and drop by a teaspoonful on waxed paper.
- Cool for 1 to 2 hours

CHOCOLATE OATMEAL COOKIES

Preparing
10 Minutes

Cooking
10 Minutes

Serve
1-2 hours

INGREDIENTS

- 2 cups Sugar
- ½ cup Cocoa
- ½ cup Milk
- ¼ lb Butter
- 3 cups Oats
- ½ cup Peanut Butter
- 1 teaspoon Vanilla

DIRECTIONS

COOK OVER FIRE UNTIL MIXTURE BOILS FOR 1 MINUTE

- 2 cups sugar
- ½ cup cocoa
- ½ cup milk
- ¼ lb butter

THEN REMOVE AND ADD:

- 3 cups Oats
- ½ cup Peanut Butter
- 1 teaspoon Vanilla
- Spoon by teaspoonful onto wax paper

CHOCOLATE OATMEAL COOKIES

INGREDIENTS

- 2 cups sugar
- ½ cup cocoa
- ½ cup milk
- ¼ lb butter
- 3 cups oats
- ½ cup peanut butter
- 1 teaspoon vanilla

DIRECTIONS

- Cook over heat for 1 minute after reaching boiling stage all ingredients except oats and peanut butter
- Mix in oats and peanut butter with vanilla
- Mix together well and drop on wax paper by spoonsful

BACHELOR BUTTON COOKIES

INGREDIENTS

- ¾ cup butter
- 1 cup dark brown sugar, packed
- 1 egg
- 2 cups flour
- 1 teaspoon baking soda
- ½ cup coconut
- ½ cup chopped nuts
- ½ cup chopped candied cherries

DIRECTIONS

- Cream butter and then add sugar.
- Stir in egg and beat well.
- Sift flour, and soda and add to cream mixture. Mix well.
- Fold in coconut, nuts, and cherries.
- Drop by teaspoonful onto a cookie sheet.
- Bake at 350 degrees for 12 to 15 minutes.

SUGAR COOKIES

INGREDIENTS

- 1 ½ cup sifted flour
- 1 ½ teaspoons baking powder
- ½ teaspoon salt
- ½ cup butter
- 1 egg
- 1 teaspoon vanilla
- 1 teaspoon Milk

DIRECTIONS

- Cream butter, sugar, egg, vanilla, and milk together.
- Mix dry ingredients together and slowly add to the creamed mixture.
- Mix thoroughly to make a stiff dough.
- Roll out on lightly floured board and cut with a cookie cutter.
- Place on an ungreased cookie sheet and sprinkle with sugar.
- Bake in a moderate oven 375 degrees for 8 to 10 minutes.

SUGAR JUMBLE COOKIES

INGREDIENTS

- ½ cup Shortening
- ½ cup Sugar
- 1 Egg
- 1 teaspoon Vanilla
- 1 1/8 cup Flour
- ¼ teaspoon Baking Soda
- ½ teaspoon Salt

DIRECTIONS

- Mix all ingredients together.
- Drop teaspoonfuls on a greased pan.
- Bake at 375 degrees for 8 to 10 minutes.

Oatmeal Icebox Cookies

Preparing
20-25 Minutes/Overnight

Cooking
10-12 Minutes

Serve
30 Minutes

INGREDIENTS

- 1 cup margarine or butter
- 1 cup brown sugar
- 1 cup white sugar
- 2 eggs (beaten)
- 1 ½ cups sifted flour
- 1 teaspoon salt
- 1 teaspoon baking soda
- 3 cups quick oats
- ½ cup finely chopped nuts

DIRECTIONS

- Cream sugar and margarine or butter together.
- Add eggs and mix thoroughly.
- Mix dry ingredients together and slowly add to wet ingredients mixing thoroughly.
- Add oats and nuts and mix well.
- Shape into rolls. Roll in waxed paper.
- Place in refrigerator overnight.
- Slice thinly and bake at 350 degrees for about 12 minutes on a lightly greased cookie sheet.

MOLASSES COOKIES

INGREDIENTS

- 1 cup Molasses
- ½ cup Shortening
- 1 teaspoon Baking Soda
- 2 ¼ cups Flour
- 1 ¾ teaspoonful Baking Powder
- 1 teaspoon Salt
- 1 ½ teaspoonful Ginger

DIRECTIONS

- Heat Molasses until it begins to boil. Remove from heat.
- Add shortening and baking soda and keep stirring.
- Blend the remaining ingredients and stir in gradually.
- Chill the dough and roll it thin.
- Cut out the cookies and place them on a lightly greased cookie sheet.
- Bake for 5 to 7 minutes in a 350-degree oven.
- Be Careful not to Over Bake!

OATMEAL COOKIES

INGREDIENTS

- 1 cup Shortening
- 1 teaspoon Nutmeg
- 1 ½ cups Brown Sugar, packed
- 2/3 cup Milk
- 2 cups Flour, sifted
- 3 cups Oats
- ½ teaspoon Salt
- 1 cup Raisins
- 1 teaspoon Baking Powder
- 1 cup chopped Dates
- 1 teaspoon Cloves
- 1 teaspoon Cinnamon

DIRECTIONS

- Cream shortening and sugar.
- Sift dry ingredients together and add alternately with milk to creamed mixture.
- Add oats and raisins and mix thoroughly.
- Drop by teaspoonful onto a greased cookie sheet.
- Bake at 375 degrees for 12 minutes.

CARNIVAL COOKIES

INGREDIENTS

- ¾ cup Shortening
- 1 cup Brown Sugar
- 1 cup white Sugar
- 2 Eggs
- 1 teaspoon Baking Soda
- 1 teaspoon Baking Powder
- 2 cups Flour
- 1 cup Raisin Bran Cereal
- 1 cup Quick Oats
- ½ cup Peanut Butter
- 1 teaspoon Vanilla

DIRECTIONS

- Mix together the shortening, sugar, and eggs.
- Mix all dry ingredients together and slowly add to the creamed mixture.
- Mix thoroughly then add cereal, oats, peanut butter, and vanilla.
- Bake at 350 degrees for 10 to 12 minutes on an ungreased cookie sheet.

ALLSPICE HERMITS

INGREDIENTS

- 1 ½ cups Flour
- ¼ cup Milk
- 2 teaspoons Baking Powder
- ½ cup chopped Nuts
- ½ teaspoon Salt
- 1 cup seedless Raisins
- 1 teaspoon Allspice
- 1 teaspoon Cinnamon
- ½ teaspoon Cloves
- ½ cup Shortening
- 1 cup Brown Sugar, packed
- 1 Egg, beaten

DIRECTIONS

- Mix and sift flour, baking powder, salt and spices.
- Cream shortening and sugar until light and fluffy.
- Add egg, raisins and nuts and mix well.
- Add dry ingredients alternately with milk.
- Drop teaspoonful 2' apart on well-greased cookie sheet.
- Bake at 375 degrees for 12 to 15 minutes.

Notes

HOLIDAY LIZZIES

Preparing
20 Minutes

Cooking
20-25 Minutes

Serve
10 Minutes

INGREDIENTS

- ½ cup Brown Sugar
- 1 lb. whole Pecans
- ¼ cup Oleo
- ¾ lb. seeded Raisins
- 2 Eggs (well beaten)
- 1 teaspoon Cinnamon
- ½ cup Whiskey
- ¼ teaspoon Nutmeg
- ½ teaspoon Baking Soda
- ¼ teaspoon Cloves
- ½ tablespoon sweet Milk
- ½ lb. Candied Cherries
- 1 ½ cups Flour
- 2 slices Candied Pineapple

DIRECTIONS

- Cream sugar and butter.
- Add well-beaten eggs.
- Add and mix well 1 cup flour, all fruits and nuts.
- Add the remaining flour to the mixture.
- Dissolve baking soda in sweet milk and then add whiskey to all fruit and nut mixture.
- Drop on a greased cookie sheet by teaspoonful.
- Bake slowly in a 325-degree oven for 20 to 25 minutes.
- Makes 4 dozen.

JUNE'S COOKIES

INGREDIENTS

- 2 cups Special K cereal
- ½ cup Coconut
- ½ cup Sugar
- ½ cup white Karo
- ½ cup Peanut Butter

DIRECTIONS

- Mix sugar and Karo together in a heavy pan.
- Add peanut butter and bring to a boil.
- Add cereal and coconut.
- Drop by teaspoonful onto waxed paper.

COCONUT MACROONS

INGREDIENTS

- 2 Egg Whites
- ¾ cup Sugar
- Dash Salt
- 1 teaspoon Vanilla
- ¼ cup Flour
- 7 oz pkg Coconut

DIRECTIONS

- Preheat oven to 325 degrees.
- Line 2 cookie sheets with foil.
- In a medium bowl mix egg whites, sugar, salt, and vanilla.
- Add flour and blend well.
- Fold in coconut.
- Drop a teaspoonful on a cookie sheet 1 inch apart.
- Bake for 15 to 20 minutes.
- Cool on cookie sheet.
- Remove and store in a tightly covered cookie jar.

PRALINE COOKIES

INGREDIENTS

- 1 cup Brown Sugar
- 2 sticks Oleo
- 1 cup Pecans
- Graham Crackers

DIRECTIONS

- Melt together brown sugar and butter and cook for 5 minutes.
- Stir in pecans.
- Line a large cookie sheet with graham crackers.
- Pour mixture over crackers.
- Bake for 10 minutes at 350 degrees.

MEXICAN COOKIES

INGREDIENTS

- ¼ cup oleo, softened
- 12 corn or flour tortillas
- ½ cup sugar
- 2 teaspoons ground cinnamon
- 1 teaspoon grated lemon peel
- 1 square semi-sweet chocolate, grated
- Chilled grape clusters
- Sliced apples
- Kiwi fruit

DIRECTIONS

- Butter tortillas, place on ungreased baking sheets.
- Mix sugar, cinnamon, and lemon peel.
- Sprinkle on tortillas.
- Bake in a slow oven at 325 degrees for 15 minutes.
- Remove from oven and sprinkle with grated chocolate.
- Serve with grapes, apples, and kiwi fruit.

SIX IN ONE COOKIES

Preparing
30-45 Minutes

 **Cooking**
10-12 Minutes

 **Serve**
10 Minutes

INGREDIENTS

- 2 cups Butter
- 1 cup white Sugar
- 1 cup light Brown Sugar
- 1 teaspoon Vanilla
- 2 Eggs (beaten)
- 1 teaspoon Baking Soda
- ½ teaspoon Salt
- 4 cups Flour
- ½ cup Nuts to a roll or ¼ cup Candied Fruit.
- 1 block of 1 oz unsweetened Chocolate (melted)

DIRECTIONS

- Cream butter and gradually add sugar.
- Cream until light and fluffy.
- Add eggs and vanilla and mix well.
- Sift flour, baking soda, and salt.
- Gradually add to the cream mixture beating well after each addition.
- Divide dough into 6 equal parts.
- You can use whatever you want such as nuts, coconut, and candied fruit.
- Roll the dough out and add whatever filling you want and then pour on chocolate.
- Shape dough into rolls about 1 ½ inches in diameter.
- Wrap and freeze.
- To bake –slice frozen dough 18" thick.
- Bake on a lightly greased cookie sheet in a 375-degree oven for 10 to 12 minutes.

THE AIRPLANE

I remember my uncles telling this story with my Momma and it is so funny. You wonder about the time they grew up and the life that they had to live, during the depression, the war, and the way they survived it all.
They survived by loving each other, enjoying the simple things of life, and the pure laughter of events. This is one of those events.
My grandfather was a cotton farmer. They would move to where he could plant and work the cotton for a percentage of its worth when harvested. It was at one of these locations that *'The Airplane'* Incident occurred.

During World War II Lamar County had an active Army Camp called Camp Maxey and at this camp they kept prisoners of war. Planes flew in and out all day and all night long.

One afternoon my Uncle Pill was sitting on the back porch of their house in Brushy Mound when he heard a loud noise. He looked up to see a plane crashing in their back pasture. My other Uncle WA was also home at the time. They did not have a truck or even a car but they had a tractor. They jumped on the tractor and off they went to the crash site. The plane was on fire and in several pieces. The pilot was hurt but not bad so they loaded him up in the tractor and off they went. There was no phone at the house.
So they drove the tractor several miles down the farm road to a little country store that actually had the only working phone in that area. My uncle called Camp Maxey and talked with the person in charge and told them of the crash and that the pilot was okay but the plane was not.
They took the pilot back to the house where my grandmother dressed his cuts and gave him food. They waited for what they thought would be 1 car to come and pick up the pilot. To their astonishment not only was there a car but several trucks and trailers. The army started that day to retrieve all of the plane's parts and my uncles said it was the most excitement any of the farmers had for many days.

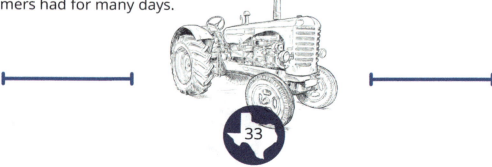

CAKES

A place to write new recipes or create your own.

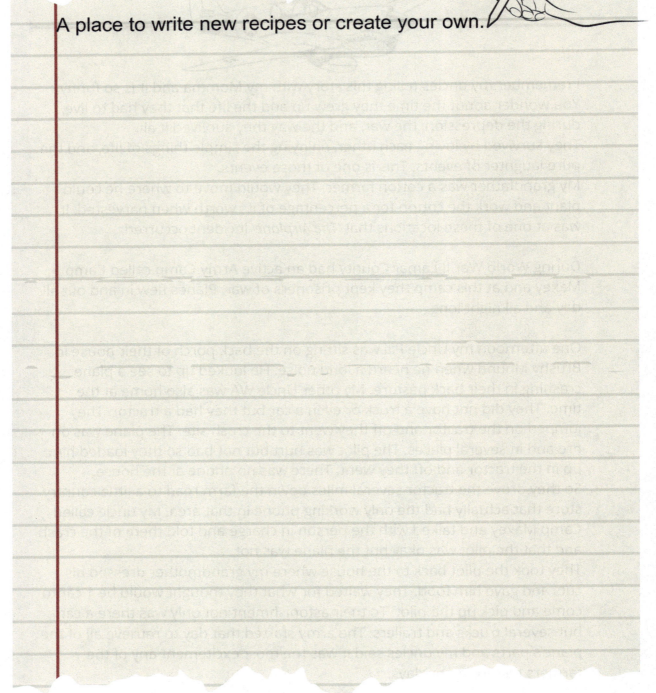

FRUIT COCKTAIL CAKE

Preparing
20 Minutes

Cooking
37 Minutes

Serve
10 Minutes

INGREDIENTS

- 2 cups unsifted flour
- 1 ½ cups sugar
- ¼ cup brown sugar
- 1 teaspoon salt
- 1 teaspoon baking soda
- 2 whole eggs
- 1 large can fruit cocktail (juice and all)
- 1 cup nuts, chopped

FILLING:

- 1 stick oleo
- ½ can Carnation Milk
- 2/3 cup white sugar

DIRECTIONS

- Mix flour, baking soda, sugars, and salt together.
- Add eggs, a fruit cocktail, and nuts.
- Dump altogether in an ungreased pan and bake at 350 degrees for 35 minutes.
- Leave in pan and add filling

FILLING:

- Boil for 2 minutes.
- Pour over the cake.
- Add 1 cup coconut while warm
- Cut in squares

SUGAR CAKE

INGREDIENTS

- 1 cup sugar
- 2/3 cup lard (solid oil)
- 1 ½ cup Milk
- 2 teaspoons baking powder
- 3 eggs

DIRECTIONS

- Mix all together
- Bake in a square pan at 350 degrees for about 30 minutes

SOUR CREAM COFFEE CAKE

INGREDIENTS

- 2 sticks oleo
- 1 teaspoon vanilla
- 2 cups sugar
- 2 cups flour
- 2 eggs
- 1 cup sour cream
- 1 teaspoon baking powder
- ¼ teaspoon salt

FILLING:
- ½ cup pecans, chopped
- 2 tablespoons brown sugar
- 1 teaspoon cinnamon

DIRECTIONS

- Cream together oleo and sugar.
- Add all other ingredients beating until well-blended
- Arrange ½ batter in a greased and floured tube pan
- Sprinkle filling on top
- Put remaining batter over filling
- Bake at 350 degrees for 1 hour

CHOCOLATE CAKE

INGREDIENTS

- 2 cups Flour
- 1 ½ cups Sugar
- 1 teaspoon Salt
- 1 ½ teaspoon Baking Soda
- 1 teaspoon Baking Powder
- 3 or 4 tablespoons Chocolate
- 1 teaspoon Vanilla
- 1 cup hot Water
- 1 cup Mayonnaise

DIRECTIONS

- Mix all dry ingredients together
- Add water, vanilla and mayonnaise
- Cook in floured pan at 350 degrees for 30 minutes

BABY FOOD CAKE

INGREDIENTS

- 1 cup oil (Olive, Canola, Wesson, etc.)
- 2 cups sugar
- 3 eggs
- 2 cups flour
- 1 teaspoon baking soda
- 1 teaspoon cinnamon
- 1 teaspoon nutmeg
- 1 jar apricot baby food
- 1 jar prune baby food
- 1 cup pecans

DIRECTIONS

- Mix together oil, sugar and eggs.
- Add dry mixture and mix all well
- Add baby food and pecans
- Bake in a greased and floured Bundt pan for 1 hour at 350 degrees

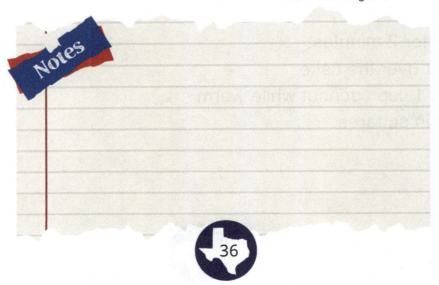

ONE EGG CAKE

INGREDIENTS

- 1 egg
- ¾ cup sugar
- 1 tablespoon baking powder
- ½ teaspoon Salt
- 2 cups Cake Flour
- 1 cup Milk

DIRECTIONS

- Mix together flour, baking powder, sugar and salt
- Add egg and milk and mix in a mixer for 3 minutes
- Pour in pan and cook at 350 degrees for 30 minutes

ORANGE POUND CAKE

INGREDIENTS

- 1 cup Shortening
- 3 cups Flour
- 2 cups Sugar
- ¾ cup Buttermilk
- 4 Eggs
- 1 teaspoon Baking Soda
- ½ oz bottle of Orange flavor
- 1 teaspoon Vinegar
- ½ teaspoon Yellow food coloring
- 1 teaspoon Salt
- 1 teaspoon Butter flavoring

DIRECTIONS

- Cream shortening and sugar.
- Add eggs one at a time and mix well.
- Add flavor, color, and salt.
- Sift flour and add to the mixture alternately with buttermilk.
- Mix baking soda and vinegar in a small bowl
- Add to the above mixture and blend all well.
- Bake in a tube pan in a slow oven at 325 degrees about 1 hour and 5 minutes
- **DO NOT OVERBAKE!!!**

PINEAPPLE CAKE

INGREDIENTS

CAKE:
- ½ cup Pineapple
- 1 box white or yellow Cake mix
- 1 pkg Lemon Jell-O
- 4 Eggs
- ½ cup Water
- 2/3 cup Wesson Oil

ICING:
- ½ stick Oleo
- 1 box powdered Sugar
- ½ cup Pineapple Juice

DIRECTIONS

CAKE:
- Mix all together and beat well.
- Bake at 350 degrees for 30 to 35 minutes until the knife in the center of the cake comes out clean.

ICING:
- Mix well and spread over cooled cake

CHOCOLATE POUND CAKE

INGREDIENTS

- ½ lb Butter
- ½ teaspoon baking powder
- ½ cup shortening
- ½ teaspoon salt
- 3 cups sugar
- 4 tablespoons cocoa
- 5 eggs
- 1 cup milk
- 3 cups flour
- 1 teaspoon vanilla

DIRECTIONS

- Cream together butter and shortening.
- Add sugar and eggs.
- Sift dry ingredients together and add vanilla.
- Add alternately with milk the creamed mixture.
- Bake in tube pan at 325 degrees for about 1 hour

BANANA CAKE

INGREDIENTS

- 3 cups Cake flour
- ¾ cup milk
- 2 teaspoons baking soda
- 2 eggs, slightly beaten
- 1 cup lard
- 2 cups sugar
- 1 ½ cups mashed ripe bananas

CREAM CHEESE FROSTING

- 1 (3 oz) package of cream cheese
- 3 cups powdered sugar
- ¼ cup sweet cream
- ½ teaspoon Vanilla

DIRECTIONS

- Line the bottom of 3 x 9-inch cake pans with waxed paper
- Sift together flour and soda
- Cream lard thoroughly
- Add sugar gradually and cream until light and fluffy
- Add 2 tablespoons milk, then eggs
- Add dry ingredients and remaining milk alternately, beating thoroughly after each addition
- Fold mashed bananas into batter and pour into cake pans
- Bake in a moderate oven at 350 degrees for 25 to 30 minutes

Frost with cream cheese frosting

- Cream the cheese
- Add powdered sugar
- Thin with cream and flavor with vanilla
- Beat until thick enough to spread

FRUIT CAKE

INGREDIENTS

- 2 cups sugar
- 1 cup chopped nuts
- 1 cup shortening
- 1 cup chopped raisins
- 3 eggs, beaten
- 1 cup coconut
- 1 cup buttermilk
- 3 ½ cups flour
- 1 teaspoon baking soda
- 1 cup blackberry jelly

FILLING

- 2 cups sugar
- 1 ½ cups coconut
- 1 ½ cups sweet milk
- 3 tablespoons flour
- 1 lemon
- 1 cup chopped nuts
- 1 orange

DIRECTIONS

- Cream shortening and sugar and eggs.
- Add baking soda to buttermilk then add to the first mixture
- Alternate with flour until well mixed then add the remaining ingredients
- Cook in 3 to 4-layer pans

FILLING:

- Mix sugar and flour.
- Cut lemon and orange into pieces.
- ***Do not use the rind.***
- Cook together until thick, like honey.
- Add coconut and cook for 2 minutes longer.
- Add nuts
- ***DO NOT COOK IN ALUMINUM PANS***

Notes

HONEY GINGERBREAD

INGREDIENTS

- 1 cup Oleo, softened
- 2 teaspoons ginger
- 1 ½ cups honey
- 1 ½ teaspoon baking soda
- 1 egg
- 1 teaspoon cinnamon
- 2 ½ cups Flour
- ¾ cup boiling Water

DIRECTIONS

- Preheat oven to 350 degrees.
- Grease 2 (8 ½ X 4 ½) Loaf Pan
- In a bowl cream together butter and ½ cup honey.
- Mix in egg.
- In a medium bowl blend together flour, ginger, baking soda, and cinnamon.
- In a small bowl blend together the remaining honey with the boiling water.
- With the mixer running, add 1/3 dry mixture to the cream mixture
- Then add the liquid mixture. Do this until all is added and mixed well.
- Turn batter into prepared pans.
- Bake until a toothpick inserted into the center comes out clean 40 to 50 minutes

FRUIT CAKE

INGREDIENTS

- ½ cup sugar
- ¾ cup oleo
- 1 ½ cup raisins
- 1 ¾ cup nuts
- 1 ½ teaspoon Baking Soda (if using sweet milk use baking powder)
- 3 cups flour
- ¾ teaspoon cinnamon
- ¾ teaspoon cloves
- ¾ teaspoon Allspice
- ¾ teaspoon Nutmeg
- 1 ½ cups sour milk or sweet milk

DIRECTIONS

- Mix all together.
- Put in a greased and floured tube pan
- Bake in a slow oven
- 325 degrees for several hours

Notes

22 MINUTE CAKE

INGREDIENTS

- 2 cups flour
- ½ cup buttermilk
- 2 cups sugar
- 2 Eggs
- 1 stick margarine
- 1 teaspoon baking soda
- 1 cup water
- 1 teaspoon vanilla
- ½ cup shortening
- 1 teaspoon cinnamon
- 3 ½ teaspoons cocoa

DIRECTIONS

- Combine sugar and flour in a large bowl.
- Do not use a mixer.
- In a saucepan, combine margarine, water, shortening, and cocoa.
- Bring to a boil and pour over the mixture.
- Combine remaining ingredients add to batter and blend thoroughly.
- Pour into a 12 x 18-inch greased and floured pan.
- Bake 20 minutes at 400 degrees.

LEMON CHEESE CAKE

INGREDIENTS

- ½ cup oleo, melted
- 1 cup sugar
- 1 pkg lemon gelatin
- 3 tablespoons lemon juice
- ¾ cup hot water
- 1 lg can evaporated milk
- 1 large pkg cream cheese
- ¾ lb graham cracker crumbs

DIRECTIONS

- Mix crumbs and oleo and press into the bottom of 13 x 9 x 2 pan.
- Reserve enough crumbs to sprinkle over the top of the cake.
- Set aside.
- Dissolve gelatin in hot water.
- Refrigerate until slightly congealed.
- Blend cheese and sugar until smooth and creamy.
- Combine with gelatin.
- Add lemon juice and then whip in evaporated milk.
- Pour over graham cracker crust
- Chill overnight

LEMON POUND CAKE

INGREDIENTS

- 3 cups flour
- 1 cup buttermilk
- ½ cup cornstarch
- ¼ teaspoon baking soda
- 3 cups sugar
- 1 cup buttermilk
- 6 eggs
- 1 cup Crisco
- 3 tablespoons lemon extract

DIRECTIONS

- Sift flour in a bowl.
- Remove ½ cup of flour
- Add ½ cup cornstarch.
- Beat egg whites until stiff and dry.
- Cream egg yolks, sugar, and Crisco until light and fluffy.
- Add buttermilk and soda and mix thoroughly.
- Pour in the flour mixture and beat until creamy.
- Add lemon extract.
- Fold in egg whites
- Pour into a large tube pan
- Bake at 350 degrees for 2 hours.

WHITE CAKE

INGREDIENTS

- 2 ½ cups sifted flour
- 3 teaspoons baking powder
- ¼ teaspoon salt
- ¼ cup shortening
- 1 ½ cups sugar
- 2 eggs
- 1 cup milk
- 1 teaspoon vanilla

DIRECTIONS

- Combine flour, baking powder, and salt and sift together.
- Add shortening, sugar, milk and vanilla.
- Beat for 2 minutes.
- Add eggs and beat for 2 minutes more
- Bake at 350 degrees for 30 minutes in a layer cake pan

JAM NUT CAKE

INGREDIENTS

- 1 cup butter
- 1 cup jam
- 1 ½ cup buttermilk
- 2 cups nuts
- 1 level teaspoon baking soda
- 3 cups flour
- 1 teaspoon Allspice
- 2 cups sugar
- 1 teaspoon cinnamon
- ½ teaspoon salt
- 1 teaspoon vanilla

ICING:

- 1 ½ cups sugar
- 1 ½ cup Sweet Milk
- 2 tablespoons flour
- 1 teaspoon vanilla

DIRECTIONS

- Cream sugar and shortening.
- Add buttermilk with soda to dissolve.
- Sift flour and spices.
- Add to creamed mixture until well mixed.
- Bake in layer pans or Bundt cake pan at 350 degrees for 30 to 35 minutes (layer pans)-40 to 45 minutes for bundt pan or until knife placed in center of cake comes out clean.

ICING:

- Cook together until thick.
- Remove from heat and beat in 2 tablespoons flour.
- Add 1 teaspoon vanilla and beat until thick enough to spread.

NOTHING CAKE

INGREDIENTS

- 1 cup Brown Sugar
- 3 Eggs
- 1 cup Coconut
- 1 box Bisquick Mix
- 1 cup Pecans

DIRECTIONS

- Bake at 25 to 30 minutes at 350 degrees

GINGER CAKE

INGREDIENTS
- 2 cups flour, sifted
- ½ cup sugar
- 1/3 cup shortening/butter
- ½ teaspoon baking soda
- 2 teaspoons baking powder
- 1 egg
- ½ teaspoon salt
- 2/3 cup molasses
- 2 teaspoons Ginger
- ¾ cup sour milk
- ½ teaspoon cinnamon
- ½ teaspoon Allspice

DIRECTIONS
- Sift together baking powder, baking soda, salt and spices.
- Cream butter and sugar.
- Continue to cream until light and fluffy.
- Add eggs and beat.
- Add Molasses
- Add flour mixture alternately with milk and beat until well mixed.
- Bake in a greased 9 x 9 x 2 pan at 350 degrees for 50 to 60 minutes

ORANGE CHIFFON CAKE

INGREDIENTS
- 2 ¼ cups flour, sifted
- 1 ½ cups sugar
- 3 teaspoons baking powder
- 1 teaspoon salt
- ½ cup cooking oil
- 5 unbeaten egg yolks (**save egg whites for later**)
- 2 tablespoons grated orange rinds
- Juice of 2 oranges plus Water to make ¾ cup
- ½ teaspoon Cream of Tarter.

DIRECTIONS
- Mix flour, sugar, baking powder, and salt

Make a well and add in order:
- ½ cup cooking Oil
- 5 unbeaten Egg Yolks(save egg whites for later)
- 2 tablespoons grated Orange rinds
- Juice of 2 Oranges plus Water to make ¾ cup
- BEAT UNTIL SMOOTH
- Whip 1 cup egg whites till very stiff with ½ teaspoon cream of tarter.
- Fold them gently together. ***DO NOT STIR!***
- Bake in an ungreased tube pan for 65 to 70 minutes at 350 degrees.

MISSISSIPPI MUD CAKE

INGREDIENTS
- 2 cups sugar
- 1 teaspoon vanilla
- 4 eggs
- 1/3 cup cocoa
- 2 sticks oleo, melted
- 1 cup Pecans
- 1 ½ cups Flour
- 1 cup Coconut

FROSTING:
- 1 stick oleo
- 1 teaspoon vanilla
- 6 tablespoons milk
- 1 box powdered sugar
- 1/3 cup cocoa
- 1 cup pecans

DIRECTIONS
- Cream all ingredients together
- Put in a baking dish and bake at 350 degrees for 30 minutes.
- As soon as the cake is done spread 1 jar of marshmallow cream on top of the cake
- Let it cool

FROSTING:
- Mix together and put on top of marshmallow cream

PRUNE CAKE

INGREDIENTS
- 2 cups sugar
- 1 tablespoon baking soda
- 1 cup oil
- 1 cup buttermilk
- 3 eggs
- 1 cup chopped nuts
- 1 cup cooked prunes
- 2 cups flour
- ½ teaspoon salt
- 1 teaspoon Allspice
- 1 teaspoon cinnamon
- 1 teaspoon nutmeg

DIRECTIONS
- SIFT TOGETHER: Flour, Salt, Allspice Cinnamon, Nutmeg
- Add the baking soda to the buttermilk.
- Add dry ingredients alternately with the milk and sugar mixture.
- Add nuts and prunes.
- Bake in a tube pan at 350 degrees for 1 hour.

FRUIT COCKAIL CAKE

INGREDIENTS
- 1 ½ sticks oleo
- 1 can Fruit Cocktail
- 1 ½ cups sugar
- 1 can Pineapple
- 2 cups Flour
- ½ teaspoon Salt
- 2 Eggs
- 2 teaspoons Baking Soda

ICING:
- 1 stick Oleo
- 1 cup Sugar
- 1 cup evaporated Milk
- 3 Egg Yolks

DIRECTIONS
- Cook at 350 degrees for 35 to 40 Minutes or until a knife placed in the center of the cake comes out clean

ICING:
- Cook until thick.
- Let cool and out on the cake

ORANGE SLICE CAKE

INGREDIENTS
- 1 cup butter
- 1 lb. dates, chopped
- 2 cups sugar
- 2 cups chopped nuts
- 4 eggs
- 1 cup flake coconut
- 1 teaspoon baking soda
- 1 cup buttermilk
- 3 ½ cups flour
- 1 lb Orange Slices, chopped

GLAZE FOR ORANGE SLICE CAKE
- 1 cup fresh orange juice
- 2 cups powdered sugar

DIRECTIONS
- Cream butter and sugar until smooth.
- Add eggs one at a time and beat well after each egg.
- Dissolve soda in buttermilk and add to the creamed mixture.
- Place flour in a large bowl and add dates, orange slices, and nuts.
- Stir until all mixed and then add to creamed mixture.
- Then add coconut.
- Mix well.
- This makes a very stiff dough that should be mixed with hands to make sure all is mixed well.
- Put in a greased and floured 13 x 9 x 3-inch cake pan.
- Bake at 250 degrees for 2 ½ hours to 3 hours

GLAZE FOR ORANGE SLICE CAKE
- Combine orange juice and powdered sugar and pour over hot cake.
- Let stand in the pan overnight

THE LOCKE CLAN

FRUIT CAKE

INGREDIENTS

- ½ lb butter
- 1 sack marshmallows
- 1 box raisins
- 1 jar candied cherries
- 1 box Graham Crackers
- 2 cups nuts

DIRECTIONS

- Melt butter and marshmallows.
- Stir to keep from sticking.
- Stir in raisins
- Add graham crackers a few at a time.
- Stir in cherries and juice.
- Work in the nuts by hand.
- Make into square cakes

DEVIL'S FOOD CAKE

INGREDIENTS

- 1 ½ cup sugar
- ½ cup shortening
- 1 cup buttermilk
- 1 egg
- 1 cup cocoa
- ½ teaspoon baking soda
- 1 teaspoon vanilla
- 1 ½ cups flour

DIRECTIONS

- Bake at 350 degrees for 35 minutes or until a knife placed in center of the cake comes out clean

CARROT FRUIT CAKE

INGREDIENTS

- 3 cups flour, sifted
- 2 teaspoons cinnamon
- 2 teaspoons baking powder
- 1 teaspoon salt
- 2 teaspoons baking soda
- 1 ½ cups salad Oil
- 2 cups sugar
- 4 eggs
- 3 cups finely grated carrots
- 1 cup chopped mixed candied fruit
- 1 cup chopped pitted dates
- 1 cup raisins
- 1 ½ cups coarsely chopped nuts

DIRECTIONS

- SIFT TOGETHER: Flour, Cinnamon, Baking Powder, Salt, Baking Soda
- SET ASIDE
- COMBINE: Salad Oil, Sugar, and Eggs.
- Beat well after each addition until light and fluffy.
- Gradually add dry ingredients mixing until smooth.
- ADD: Carrots, Candied Fruit, Dates, Raisins, and Nuts
- Mix well and spoon into a greased 10-inch tube pan.
- Bake at 350 degrees for 1 ½ hours

HEAVENLY PINEAPPLE NUT CAKE

INGREDIENTS

- 4 ¾ cups flour
- 5 eggs, beaten
- 2 tablespoons baking powder
- 1 cup mashed bananas
- 1 tablespoon baking soda
- 1 pint chopped pecans
- 1 ½ cups brown sugar
- 1 teaspoon vanilla
- 1 teaspoon salt
- ½ cup shortening
- 1 large can crushed pineapple
- ½ cup butter

DIRECTIONS

- Blend sifted dry ingredients with shortening and butter until the texture of coarse caramel.
- Stir in the next 4 ingredients.
- Fold in nuts.
- Pour the cake mixture into a greased pan.
- Bake in a moderately hot oven, 350 degrees for 40 minutes or until the toothpick inserted comes out clean.

BRAZIL NUT CAKE

INGREDIENTS

- 3 cups Brazil Nuts
- 1 lb whole pitted dates
- 1 lb Maraschino Cherries, drained
- 2/3 cup flour
- 2/3 cup sugar
- 3 eggs, beaten
- 1 teaspoon vanilla

DIRECTIONS

- Mix flour, sugar, eggs and vanilla together.
- Then add nuts, dates and cherries.
- Mix all with hands.
- Pack in greased wax paper lined loaf pan
- Bake at 300 degrees for 1 hour

JUDY'S CAKE

INGREDIENTS

- 2 cups flour
- 1 1/3 cups sugar
- 3 teaspoons baking powder
- 2 eggs
- 1 cup milk
- ½ cup oleo
- 1 teaspoon vanilla

ICING:
- 1 box powdered sugar
- 1 egg
- ¾ cup butter

DIRECTIONS

- Mix all ingredients together.
- Put in a long baking pan.
- Bake at 350 degrees for 30 to 35 minutes.

ICING:
- Mix together and put on the cake

LIGHTLY LEMON COFFEE CAKE

INGREDIENTS

- 2 tablespoons vinegar
- 2 teaspoons baking powder
- 7/8 cup can milk
- ½ teaspoon salt
- 1 teaspoon baking soda
- ½ cup brown sugar, packed
- ½ cup oleo
- 1 tablespoon cinnamon
- 2 eggs, well beaten
- 1 cup powdered sugar
- 1 teaspoon lemon rind
- 1 ¾ cup flour

DIRECTIONS

- Combine vinegar and milk in a bowl and stir in baking soda.
- Cream oleo and sugar until fluffy.
- Add eggs and lemon rind and beat well.
- Sift flour, baking powder, and salt together.
- Add alternately with milk mixture beating well.
- Mix in brown sugar and cinnamon together in a small bowl.
- Spread ½ of the batter in a greased tube pan.
- Sprinkle with half of the cinnamon and brown sugar.
- Add the remaining batter and sprinkle with the rest of the cinnamon brown sugar mix.
- Bake at 350 degrees for 45 to 50 minutes

GLAZE:
- Combine lemon juice and powdered sugar.
- Spoon over cake
- Top with lemon peel, nuts and cherries

LEMON SUPREME POUND CAKE

INGREDIENTS

- 1 pkg Duncan Hines Lemon Supreme Cake Mix
- 1 pkg lemon instant pudding mix
- ½ cup Crisco oil
- 1 cup water
- 4 eggs

GLAZE

- 1 cup powdered sugar
- 2 tablespoons milk
- 2 tablespoons lemon juice

DIRECTIONS

- Blend all ingredients in a large bowl.
- Beat at medium speed for 2 minutes.
- Bake in a greased and floured 10-inch tube pan at 350 degrees for about 45 to 55 minutes until the center springs back when touched lightly.
- Cool right side up for about 25 minutes then remove from the pan

GLAZE:

- Mix together and drizzle over the cake

BLACKBERRY JAM CAKE

INGREDIENTS

- 1 ½ cups sugar
- 1 cup raisins
- 2/3 cup butter
- 1 teaspoon Cinnamon
- 4 eggs
- 1 teaspoon cloves
- 1 teaspoon baking soda
- 1 teaspoon nutmeg
- 1 cup blackberry jam
- 1 teaspoon Allspice
- 1 cup buttermilk
- 1 cup nuts
- 2 ¼ cups flour

DIRECTIONS

- Cream butter and sugar.
- Add beaten eggs.
- Sift flour once, add baking soda, and sift again.
- Add flour and milk to batter alternately.
- Then add spices, jam, and nuts, and lastly add raisins.
- Bake in four-layer pans or a long pan at 350 degrees for 35 to 40 minutes or until knife inserted in the center of the cake comes out clean.

FRESH APPLE CAKE

INGREDIENTS

- 1 teaspoon Cloves
- 2 cups chopped apples
- 1 teaspoon Nutmeg
- 2 cups sugar
- 1 teaspoon cinnamon
- 1 teaspoon baking soda
- 1 teaspoon Allspice
- ½ teaspoon salt
- 1 2/3 cup shortening or oleo
- ½ cup cold water
- 2 ½ cups flour
- 1 cup chopped pecans
- 4 eggs
- 1 teaspoon vanilla

ICING:

- 2 cups brown sugar
- 2 tablespoons butter
- 1 cup white sugar
- 1 teaspoon vanilla
- 1 cup evaporated milk
- 1 cup pecans, finely chopped

DIRECTIONS

- Cream sugar with shortening/Oleo.
- Dissolve soda in cold water.
- Sift flour and spices together.
- Add to creamed mixture.
- Bake in 4-layer pans at 350 degrees until touched
- with finger springs back.

ICING:

- Boil all ingredients until form a soft ball in cold water.
- Beat until creamy and spread on cake.

Notes

SOCK IT TO ME CAKE

INGREDIENTS
- 3 cups Brazil Nuts
- 1 lb whole pitted Dates
- 1 lb Maraschino Cherries, drained
- 2/3 cup Flour
- 2/3 cup Sugar
- 3 Eggs, beaten
- 1 teaspoon Vanilla

Glaze:
- ½ cup Powdered Sugar
- Few drops of water

DIRECTIONS
- Mix all ingredients together and pour ½ of the mixture into a greased and floured tube pan.
- THEN:
- Mix 1 tablespoon cinnamon and 2 tablespoons sugar.
- Put on top of the mixture.
- Then put rest of mixture in pan.
- Bake at 350 degrees for 50 minutes.

While the cake is hot put on the Glaze:
- ½ cup Powdered Sugar mixed with a few drops of water.
- Drizzle over cake

Notes

CRUMB COFFEE CAKE

INGREDIENTS
- 2 cups all purpose flour
- 1 teaspoon ground cinnamon
- 2 teaspoons Nescafe instant coffee powder
- ½ cup margarine
- 1 egg
- 1 cup sour cream
- 1 teaspoon baking soda
- ½ cup chopped nuts

DIRECTIONS
- Combine the first 4 ingredients, and cut in margarine with a pastry blender until crumbs are the size of large peas.
- Press half of the crumb mixture into a greased and floured 9-inch square pan.
- Combine egg, sour cream, and baking soda.
- Add the remaining crumb mixture, and stir to blend.
- Spread over mixture in pan.
- Sprinkle nuts over top.
- Bake at 350 degrees for 45 to 50 minutes.
- Let cool and cut into squares

Granny says this is good to freeze

SOPAPILLA CHEESECAKE

INGREDIENTS
- 2 cans Crescent Rolls
- 2 – 8oz cream cheese
- 1 ½ cups sugar
- 1 teaspoon vanilla

TOPPING:
- ½ cup sugar
- 1 tablespoon cinnamon
- 1 stick butter (melted)

DIRECTIONS
- Spread one can of crescent rolls on the bottom of a 9 x 13 pan.
- Blend sugar, vanilla, and cream cheese with mixer.
- Spread the cream cheese mixture on the bottom layer of the crescent rolls.
- Take the other package of crescent rolls and spread them on top of the cream cheese (seal edges together).
- Sprinkle with a mixture of toppings.
- Bake for 30 minutes at 350 degrees

RED VELVET CAKE

INGREDIENTS

- ½ cup shortening
- 3 tablespoons cocoa
- 1 ½ cups sugar
- 2 ½ cups flour
- 2 eggs
- 1 cup buttermilk
- 1 teaspoon vanilla
- 1 teaspoon salt
- 1 teaspoon butter flavoring
- 1 tablespoon Vinegar
- 1 oz Red Food Color
- 1 teaspoon Baking Soda

NO COOK ICING
(Red Velvet Cake Icing)

- 1 lb powdered Sugar
- ½ cup Shortening (or Butter)
- 1 tablespoon Vanilla
- ¼ teaspoon Butter flavoring
- ½ teaspoon Salt
- 5 tablespoons Milk

DIRECTIONS

- Cream shortening, sugar, eggs, and butter flavoring.
- Make a paste of cocoa and red food coloring. Add to the first mixture.
- Alternately add flour and buttermilk.
- Mix baking soda and vinegar in a small bowl.
- Add to batter and blend all together
- Bake in 3 X 9-inch pans for 20 to 25 minutes at 350 degrees

NO COOK ICING

- Sift sugar - Take ½ of the sugar and blend with shortening or butter, butter flavor (only if you use shortening instead of butter), and salt.
- Alternately add the rest of the sugar and enough milk to get a smooth spreading icing

OATMEAL CAKE

INGREDIENTS

- 1 ½ cups boiling water
- 1 stick butter
- 1 cup oatmeal
- 1 cup white Sugar
- 1 cup light Brown Sugar (packed)
- 2 Eggs
- 1 ¼ cups Flour
- 1 teaspoon Baking Soda
- ½ teaspoon Cinnamon

OATMEAL CAKE ICING

- 1 stick oleo
- ¾ cup sugar
- ¼ cup can milk
- 1 teaspoon Vanilla
- 1 cup Coconut
- 1 cup Pecans

DIRECTIONS

- Mix boiling water, butter, and oatmeal.
- Let stand for 20 minutes.
- Then add white sugar, brown sugar, eggs, flour, baking soda, and cinnamon
- Bake at 350 degrees for 35 minutes.

OATMEAL CAKE ICING:

- Mix oleo, sugar, and canned milk
- Then cook for 1 minute
- Add vanilla, coconut, and pecans
- Mix all together and pour over the cake.
- Put under oven broiler and let brown.

THE TRIP TO WASHINGTON

My father was in World War II and he was stationed in Washington State. My sweet Mother who had never been anywhere outside of Lamar and Fannin county took a train to Washington to be with him. I can see her now sitting in her chair telling us the story of her journey. She would start off by saying that her Father was mad and would not tell her goodbye because she was leaving him. My grandmother and aunt made bread for her to take and eat on the way because she had no money for food. She caught the train at the train station in Paris and began the long road ahead.

My Uncle WA was in the Army as well and stationed at Fort Hood at Killeen, Texas. He went AWOL to meet her train in Dallas, Texas when it stopped to pick up more passengers, to make sure that she was okay. Thank goodness understanding authorities did not throw him in the Brig when he returned!

She talks of the young man, Private who promised Uncle WA that he would make sure she was safe. He was headed to a military camp in California. In the 40's when a young man vowed he would keep someone safe that is exactly what it meant. She talked of him and how kind he was even buying her food and milk because he knew she could not. She shared her bread and her stories of her life on the farm and how she met my father. She would say that it was a long journey but it ended quicker than she thought it would and that was because of Private.

We tried to find him the year before Momma went to heaven but could not. She wanted to tell him one more time how much she appreciated him watching over her. I wonder sometimes what would have happened if we had located him, would he have taken the time once again to see her so they could talk of that journey.

CANDY

A place to write new recipes or create your own.

SPECIAL K CANDY

INGREDIENTS

- 1 cup white Karo Syrup
- 1 cup sugar
- 12 oz peanut butter
- 4 cups Special K Cereal

DIRECTIONS

- Bring White Karo and sugar to a boil and remove from stove.
- ADD peanut butter and Special K Cereal
- Stir until all cereal is covered and drop by teaspoonful onto wax paper.
- You can add nuts and coconut if you want to

MOLASSES TAFFY

INGREDIENTS

- 1 1/3 cups (15 oz) Eagle Brand Milk
- ½ cup Molasses
- 1/8 teaspoon Salt

DIRECTIONS

- Mix together milk, molasses, and salt in a saucepan
- Cook over medium heat at 250 degrees
- Pour onto wax paper
- When cool divide and wrap in small portions in waxed paper

PEANUT PATTY

INGREDIENTS

- 3 cups Sugar
- 1 cup Water
- 1 cup light Corn Syrup
- 1 lb. raw Peanuts
- 6 drops Red Food Coloring
- ¼ cup Oleo
- Pinch Salt

DIRECTIONS

- Bring sugar, water and syrup to a boil and add peanuts and
- red food coloring.
- Cook over medium flame until hard boil stage.
- Remove from flame.
- Add oleo and salt.
- Beat until mixture is thick (color should be cloudy).
- Pour onto greased cookie sheet.
- Break into pieces when cool

DIVINITY CANDY

INGREDIENTS

- 1 ½ cups sugar
- ½ cup white Karo Syrup
- ½ cup water
- 2 egg whites
- 1 cup nuts

DIRECTIONS

- 1 ½ cups Sugar
- ½ cup white Syrup
- ½ cup Water
- Cook until makes hard boil (drop small amount in cold water
- to test)
- 2 Egg Whites
- 1 cup Nuts
- Beat egg whites until stiff and then pour ½ of mixture into
- eggs.
- Beat well and then add the remainder of the mixture and
- nuts and boil.
- After it starts to pop it is ready to pour into a buttered pan

POTATO CANDY

INGREDIENTS

- 1 medium white Potato
- 2 lbs. Powder Sugar
- 1 teaspoon Vanilla
- Peanut Butter

DIRECTIONS

- Cook potato in jacket until done.
- Pull off jacket and mash.
- Add powdered sugar and stir until real thick.
- Add vanilla and stir well.
- Roll out wax paper.
- Spread peanut butter on mixture and then roll.
- Put in ice box (refrigerator) until chilled real good.
- Then slice

PEANUT BUTTER FUDGE

INGREDIENTS

- 1 cup Brown Sugar
- 1 cup White Sugar
- ½ cup evaporated Milk
- 2 tablespoons Butter
- 1 cup Marshmallow pieces
- ¾ cup Peanut Butter
- 1 teaspoon Vanilla

DIRECTIONS

- In a heavy saucepan combine sugar, milk, and butter.
- Cook until a soft ball forms in cold water, 235 degrees on a candy thermometer.
- Just before removing the pan from heat, add the remaining ingredients.
- Stir until marshmallows are almost melted
- Remove from heat and beat until the mixture begins to thicken (about 1 minute).
- Pour immediately into a buttered 8-inch square pan.
- Let cook then cut

5 MINUTE FUDGE

INGREDIENTS

- 1 cup Brown Sugar
- 1 cup White Sugar
- ½ cup evaporated Milk
- 2 tablespoons Butter
- 1 cup Marshmallow pieces (16 medium cut into pieces)
- ¾ cup Peanut Butter
- 1 teaspoon Vanilla
- 1 ½ cups Bakers Chocolate
- ½ cup Nuts

DIRECTIONS

- Mix all ingredients and bring to a boil over low heat.
- Boil for 5 minutes stirring constantly.
- Remove from fire.
- ADD: 16 medium Marshmallows (cut into small pieces)
- Stir until melted.
- Stir in chocolate, vanilla, and nuts.
- Stir until all melted.
- Pour into a buttered pan.
- Cool and cut into squares

FUDGE CANDY

INGREDIENTS

- 4 ½ cups Sugar
- 2 sticks Butter (margarine)
- 1 large can Pet Milk
- 1 lb Marshmallows
- 3 packages of Chocolate Chips
- 1 lb chopped Nuts
- 1 tablespoon Vanilla

DIRECTIONS

- Bring to boil and then boil for 7 minutes
- ADD Marshmallows
- Beat for 2 to 3 minutes
- ADD Chocolate Chips, Nuts, and Vanilla
- Pour into a buttered pan and cut into squares
- Makes 5 lbs

MAKING COCOA FUDGE

INGREDIENTS

- 2 cups Sugar
- ½ cup Cocoa
- 1 cup Milk
- 2 tablespoons Butter
- 1 teaspoon Vanilla
- ½ teaspoon Salt

DIRECTIONS

- You will need a deep saucepan and a flat buttered dish and large spoon for beating.
- Stir the sugar and the cocoa together in the saucepan.
- Add the milk a little at a time and stir until very smooth.
- Put the mixture over heat and let boil slowly.
- It makes a soft bubbly sound as if it were telling you cheerful news!
- **WHATEVER YOU DO DON'T STIR IT AFTER IT BEGINS TO BOIL OR YOUR FUDGE WILL BE SUGARY AND HARD**
- When reaches soft boil stage –pour into buttered dish and let harden before cutting into pieces.

SKILLET CANDY

INGREDIENTS
- 1 8 oz pkg Dates
- 1 stick Oleo
- 2 Eggs
- ¾ cup Sugar
- 2 cups Rice Crispies Cereal
- 1 cup Nuts, chopped
- Small pkg Coconut

DIRECTIONS
- Put dates, butter, eggs and sugar in a skillet over low heat.
- Cook 15 minutes stirring often.
- Remove from heat.
- Stir in Rice Crispies and nuts.
- Make a roll or ball and then roll in Coconut.

ORANGE – COCONUT BALLS

INGREDIENTS
- 1 lb. Vanilla Wafers (ground)
- 1 box Powdered Sugar
- 1 stick Oleo (melted and cooled)
- 1 6 oz frozen Orange Juice (let it get mushy)

DIRECTIONS
- Mix all ingredients together.
- Work with your hands and shape into small balls.
- Roll balls in Coconut or place ½ pecan piece on each ball.

NO COOK CANDY BALL

INGREDIENTS
- 1 cup creamy Peanut Butter
- 1 cup sifted Powder Sugar
- ½ cup Nuts
- 2 tablespoons softened Butter
- 1 cup Flake Coconut

DIRECTIONS
- Combine the 1st four ingredients in a mixing bowl.
- Mix well.
- Shape into ½ inch ball.
- Roll each ball in coconut.
- Chill for 1 hour in refrigerator

PEANUT PATTIES

INGREDIENTS
- 2 cups Sugar
- ½ cup Water
- ½ cup Corn Syrup
- 1 ½ cups raw Peanuts
- 1 lb. Oleo
- Dash Salt
- 1 teaspoon Vanilla
- 2 to 3 drops Red Food Coloring

DIRECTIONS
- Combine sugar, water, salt and syrup in 2 qt glass bowl.
- Bring to a boil in microwave – approximately 3 minutes.
- Stir and add peanuts.
- Return to microwave and cook 9 to 10 minutes or until soft
- boil stage – 234 degrees on baking thermometer – has been
- reached.
- Remove from microwave and add oleo, vanilla and red food
- coloring.
- Beat until creamy.
- Drop tablespoons onto wax paper.

PEANUT BRITTLE

INGREDIENTS
- 1 cups Sugar
- 3 cups raw Peanuts
- 1 cup white Syrup

DIRECTIONS
- Put together and boil until mixture turns tan and the
- peanuts start to pop.
- Turn off the fire and add one stick of oleo and 2 teaspoons
- of baking soda.
- Pour on a buttered pan.

CHOCOLATE SYRUP

INGREDIENTS

- 1 cup Sugar
- 3 tablespoons Karo syrup
- 8 tablespoons Cocoa
- ¼ cup Water

DIRECTIONS

- Cook until mixture forms a soft ball in cold water.
- Add one small can of milk (Pet, etc) and 1 teaspoon vanilla
- Will keep in the refrigerator for days

FANTASY FUDGE

INGREDIENTS

- 2 or 3 cups Sugar
- ¾ cup Oleo
- 1 small can evaporated Milk
- 2 6oz pkgs of Chocolate Chips (semi-sweet)
- 2 cups Marshmallow Cream
- 1 cup chopped Nuts
- 1 teaspoon Vanilla

DIRECTIONS

- Combine sugar, oleo and milk.
- Bring to a boil. Stir for 5 minutes over medium heat until it
- reaches soft ball stage.
- Remove from heat.
- Stir in chocolate chips and then add marshmallow cream,
- nuts and vanilla.
- Beat well until blended.
- Pour into a greased 13 x 9-inch pan.
- Cool and cut into squares

Notes

GRANNY AND POP-PA

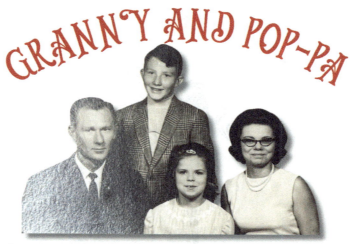

In our lives, we are fortunate to have so many wonderful people who adopt us into their families.

In 1993 Jarvis and Patricia Howard (Granny and Pop-Pa) adopted me and
my children when I married their son.

Jarvis was such a special man. He lost a leg when he was a child but that did not stop him from doing anything that he chose to do. Listening to my husband tell of adventures they would go on when he was growing up is unbelievable. Jarvis with 1 leg drove a truck with no power steering and was a 3-speed manual not automatic. He would use his cane as his second leg and sometimes when hunting would get into some tight situations! He worked 2 jobs to support his family. He was a set printer for the newspaper and also for Swaim Printing Company. He developed cancer in his "good leg" and had to have the bone replaced but that did not stop him either. While bedridden for healing he developed a new connection with people. My husband got him a 2 way radio which turned into his saving grace. He now had a way to talk and help many people on their journeys.

Pat (Granny) was quite the lady. Jarvis met her at the grocery store. My husband was a small child and she embraced him with open arms and became his Mother. Granny worked, raised 2 children, had an acre garden every year, canned vegetables, and made sure her children were involved in important activities. She had a stroke at an early age that most people would not have recovered from at that time. She was determined that she would be well and took the steps necessary to accomplish this feat. She was a wonderful cook and I learned many new recipes from her that had been carried down from not only Jarvis's mother and sister but from her family as well.
She introduced me to Enchilada Pie! Such a simple recipe but so good.
And of course, for dessert, she would make Butter Rolls, mmmm good!

On Christmas Eve each year, the activity for the afternoon was to make tamales. Each person had a job. Spread the Masa on the corn husks or shred the pork, chicken, and if they had it venison. Jarvis was responsible for adding the spices. Add the meat to the Masa and roll up the corn husk. Put in the pan andsteam. So Good!

We lost both of them way too soon but know that they are in
Heaven smiling down on us as we make new memories each year.

How to Keep a Husband...
Advice Given to Granny at Her Wedding Shower

1. Always trust him, never doubt his absence.
2. Just cook plenty of good food - the way to a man's heart is through his stomach.
3. Get up at 6 o'clock in the morning and prepare:
    3 spoons of coffee to 4 cups of water
    Add sugar and cream as needed or wanted
    Stir and drink
4. Stuff him with good things to eat.
5. That's entirely up to you!
6. Always treat him sweet and love him lots!
7. Be a good cook.
8. Treat him rough and tell him nothing and he will like you better.

ICING

A place to write new recipes or create your own.

NO COOK ICING
(RED VELVET CAKE ICING)

INGREDIENTS
- 1 lb powdered sugar
- ½ cup shortening (or Butter)
- 1 tablespoon Vanilla
- ¼ teaspoon Butter flavoring
- ½ teaspoon Salt
- 5 tablespoons Milk

DIRECTIONS
- Sift sugar
- Take ½ of the sugar and blend with shortening or butter, butter flavor (only if you use shortening instead of butter), and salt.
- Alternately add the rest of the sugar and enough milk to get a smooth spreading icing

ICING

INGREDIENTS
- 1 ½ cups Sugar
- 1 ½ cup Sweet Milk

DIRECTIONS
- Cook together until thick.
- Remove from heat and beat in 2 tablespoons flour.
- Add 1 teaspoon vanilla and beat until thick enough to spread.

7 MINUTE ICING

INGREDIENTS
- 2 egg whites
- 1/3 cup Karo syrup
- ¾ cup sugar
- 1 teaspoon Salt
- ¼ teaspoon Cream of Tarter
- 2 tablespoons Water

DIRECTIONS
- Cook syrup, sugar, salt, and water until comes to a boil.
- Beat egg whites and add to mixture along with cream of tarter.
- Beat all together until thick.

CARMEL ICING

INGREDIENTS
- ½ cup Shortening
- ¼ teaspoon Salt
- ½ cup Milk
- ½ cup Brown Sugar, packed
- 2 cups Confectioner Sugar, sifted
- ½ teaspoon Vanilla
- ½ cup Nuts, coarsely chopped

DIRECTIONS
- Melt in saucepan shortening and salt.
- Stir slowly and add milk.
- Bring to a boil, stirring constantly.
- Boil for 1 minute.
- Stir in brown sugar
- Remove from heat
- Stir in confectioners' sugar
- Set saucepan in cold water and beat until consistency is thick enough to spread.
- Stir in vanilla and nuts.

CREAM CHEESE FROSTING

INGREDIENTS
- 1 (3 oz) package of Cream Cheese
- 3 cups powdered sugar
- ¼ cup sweet cream
- ½ teaspoon vanilla

DIRECTIONS
- Thin with cream and flavor with vanilla
- Beat until thick enough to spread

ICING

INGREDIENTS
- ½ stick oleo
- 1 box powdered sugar
- ½ cup pineapple juice

DIRECTIONS
- Mix well and spread over cooled cake

FROSTING

INGREDIENTS
- 1 stick oleo
- 1 teaspoon vanilla
- 6 tablespoons milk
- 1 box powdered sugar
- 1/3 cup cocoa
- 1 cup pecans

DIRECTIONS
- Mix together and put on top of marshmallow cream

NO COOK MARSHMALLOW FROSTING

INGREDIENTS
- 2 egg whites
- ¼ teaspoon salt
- ¼ cup sugar
- ¾ cup Karo Syrup
- 1 ¼ teaspoon vanilla

DIRECTIONS
- Beat egg whites and salt with a beater until soft peaks form.
- Add sugar beating until smooth and glossy.
- Continue beating and add syrup a little at a time beating after each addition until frosting peaks.
- Fold in vanilla

Present-day Lamar County was part of Red River County during the Republic of Texas. By 1840, population growth necessitated the organization of a new county. George Washington Wright, who had served in the Third Congress of the Republic of Texas as a representative from Red River County, was a major proponent of the new county. The Fifth Congress established the new county on December 17, 1840, and named it after Mirabeau B. Lamar, who was the first Vice President and the second President of the Republic of Texas.

ICING

INGREDIENTS
- 2 cups brown sugar
- 2 tablespoons butter
- 1 cup white sugar
- 1 teaspoon vanilla
- 1 cup evaporated milk
- 1 cup pecans, finely chopped

DIRECTIONS
- Boil all ingredients until form a soft ball in cold water.
- Beat until creamy and spread on cake.

Notes

Misc Desserts

A place to write new recipes or create your own.

THANKSGIVING DELIGHT

INGREDIENTS

- 1 pkg Dream Whip, prepared as directed
- ½ cup Mayonnaise
- 1 cup Miniature Marshmallows
- 1 can whole Cranberry Sauce

DIRECTIONS

- Fold dream whip into all ingredients.
- Put in 2 lb cheese saver (store upside down)
- When ready to serve – take out and slice

HOMEMADE ICE CREAM

INGREDIENTS

- 1 can Cream
- 1 ¾ cup Sugar
- 1 tablespoon Vanilla
- 6 Eggs
- Pinch Salt

DIRECTIONS

- Mix all ingredients.
- Put in freezer packed in ice.
- Then allow to mix and set up
- Serve

VANILLA PUDDING

INGREDIENTS

- 3 Eggs
- ½ cup Sugar
- ½ cup Flour
- 2 cups Milk
- 1 teaspoon Vanilla
- 1 tablespoon Butter

DIRECTIONS

- Cook over medium heat until thick

FRUIT CUP

INGREDIENTS

- 1 can Comstock Peach filling
- 2 cans mandarin oranges, drained
- 1 can chunk pineapple, drained
- 1 pkg frozen whole strawberries
- 2 bananas, sliced

DIRECTIONS

- Toss all ingredients together
- Top with whipped topping

QUICK COBBLER

INGREDIENTS

- 4 heaping tablespoons Butter
- 1 cup Flour
- 1 cup Sugar
- 1 cup Milk
- 2 teaspoons Baking Powder
- Pinch Salt
- 2 cups or 1 can Fruit of choice (sweeten fruit before adding to mixture if needed by placing in a small saucepan and cook until sugar is melted)

DIRECTIONS

- Melt butter in the bottom of the baking dish
- Mix batter and pour over butter.
- Pour fruit over the batter and bake for about 35 minutes at 350 degrees.

CARMEL POPCORN

INGREDIENTS

- 1 cup brown sugar
- 1 cup butter
- ½ teaspoon salt
- ¼ cup white Karo Syrup
- ½ teaspoon baking soda

DIRECTIONS

- Cook first four ingredients for 5 minutes in a heavy pan.
- ADD baking soda
- Stir until foamy
- Pour over Popcorn fast!
- Stir and then pour onto waxed paper.

PARTY MIX

INGREDIENTS

- 1 box Rice Chex
- 1 box Corn Chex
- 1 bag of pretzels
- Peanuts
- Pecans
- 2 sticks, oleo, melted
- 2 tablespoons garlic salt
- 1 tablespoon Worcestershire Sauce
- 1 tablespoon Tabasco Sauce

DIRECTIONS

- Mix all together with your hands
- Bake at 250 degrees for 1 hour stirring often

VANILLA PUDDING

INGREDIENTS

- 1/3 cup shortening
- ½ cup peanut butter
- ¼ cup firmly packed brown sugar
- 1 cup granulated sugar
- 1 teaspoon vanilla
- 2 eggs
- 1 cup un-sifted flour
- 1 teaspoon baking powder
- ¼ teaspoon salt
- 1 1/3 cups coconut

DIRECTIONS

- Cream together shortening, peanut butter, and sugars until light and fluffy.
- Add vanilla and eggs and beat well.
- Mix in flour, baking powder, and salt stirring until thoroughly blended.
- Stir in coconut.
- Spread evenly in a greased 13 x 9-inch pan.
- Bake at 350 degrees for about 25 minutes or until golden brown.
- Cool and cut into bars

MICROWAVE CARMEL CORN

INGREDIENTS

- 1 cup Brown Sugar
- 1 stick Butter
- ¼ cup Corn Syrup
- ½ teaspoon Salt
- ½ teaspoon Baking Soda
- 3 to 4 qts Popped Corn

DIRECTIONS

- Combine all ingredients except baking soda and popcorn in 1 qt microwavable dish.
- Bring to a boil and then continue to cook for 2 minutes.
- Remove from microwave and stir in baking soda.
- Put popped corn in a brown grocery bag.
- Pour syrup over corn.
- Close the bag and shake.
- Cook in the bag in the microwave on high power for 1 ½ minutes.
- Shake and cook another 1 ½ minutes.
- Pour into pan and allow to cool.

BROWNIES

INGREDIENTS

- 1 cup Sugar
- 2/3 cup Shortening
- 1 cup Flour
- 2 Eggs
- 4 tablespoons Cocoa
- 1 teaspoon Vanilla
- ½ teaspoon Salt

DIRECTIONS

- Mix together and pour into baking dish.
- Bake at about 300 degrees until done (15 to 20 minutes)
- Ice with powdered sugar

BUTTERSCOTCH BROWNIES

INGREDIENTS

- 1 6oz pkg butterscotch chips
- ¼ cup oleo
- 1 cup sifted flour
- 1 teaspoon baking powder
- ¾ teaspoon salt
- 1 cup light Brown Sugar (packed)
- 2 Eggs
- ½ teaspoon Vanilla
- ½ cup Nuts

DIRECTIONS

- Melt butterscotch chips and oleo.
- Stir in light brown sugar.
- Let cool for 5 minutes.
- Stir in eggs and vanilla.
- Mix dry ingredients and then slowly stir into mixture and mix well.
- Stir in nuts.
- Spread into a 13 x 9 greased pan.
- Bake at 350 degrees for 25 minutes.
- **DO NOT OVERCOOK!**

BROWNIE PUDDING

INGREDIENTS

- 1 cup sifted flour
- 1 ¾ cup hot water
- ¾ cup sugar
- ¼ cup cocoa
- 2 teaspoons baking powder
- ¾ cup brown sugar
- ½ teaspoon salt
- ½ cup milk
- 2 tablespoons cooking oil
- 1 teaspoon vanilla
- ½ cup chopped pecans
- 2 teaspoons cocoa

DIRECTIONS

- Sift together flour, sugar, baking powder, salt, and cocoa.
- Add milk, oil, and vanilla.
- Mix until smooth.
- Stir in nuts.
- Pour into greased 8 x 8 x 2-inch baking pan.
- Combine hot water, brown sugar, and 2 teaspoons of Cocoa.
- Stir until smooth
- Then pour over the batter
- Bake at 350 degrees for about 40 minutes

Notes

PUMPKIN BARS

Preparing 20 Minutes

Cooking 30 Minutes

Serve 30 Minutes

INGREDIENTS

- 2 cups flour
- 1 can pumpkin
- 2 cups sugar
- 4 eggs
- 2 teaspoons baking powder
- ½ cup nuts
- 1 teaspoon baking soda
- ½ cup raisins
- 1 teaspoon cinnamon
- 1 cup oil
- 1 teaspoon nutmeg
- ½ teaspoon salt
- ½ teaspoon cloves

FROSTING FOR PUMPKIN BARS

- 2 cups powdered sugar
- 1/3 cup oleo
- 1-3 oz pkg cream cheese, softened
- 1 tablespoon milk
- 1 teaspoon vanilla

DIRECTIONS

- Combine all ingredients except nuts and raisins.
- Beat at low speed until moistened.
- Beat at medium speed for 2 minutes.
- Stir in nuts and raisins.
- Pour into a greased pan.
- Bake for 25 to 30 minutes.

FROSTING FOR PUMPKIN BARS

- Combine all ingredients and beat until smooth.
- Frost pumpkin bars when cooled.
- Store in refrigerator.

Breakfast, Lunch, & Dinner

Momma's made the meals and everyone ate together. No phones, no televisions, just conversations and thankfulness.

PANTHER ALMOST GOT THIS WOMAN

Once again Knox has a tale to tell.
This is the story of another panther nearly a hundred years ago and he told it this way:
In a community between Honey Grove and Bonham, two families lived on opposite sides of the Boisd'arc Creek, whose names he did not remember.
One of the women was sick and the other woman rode horseback across the bottom and the creek to visit her. She stayed later than she intended and it was evening before she started back home. The man in the family where she visited said he had better take his gun and two dogs and accompany her across the bottom, as he had heard a panther scream on the creek sometime before. But she told him she was not afraid as her horse could smell a panther at a considerable distance, and so she started out alone.
As she was crossing the creek bottom a panther sprang out of a tree at her and her horse. The frightened horse made a quick jump itself and the woman was thrown, but her riding skirt hung on the saddle horn. The panther, missing its aim at her. Landed on the horse's flanks, the horse ran with the panther trying to stay on it, and that probably saved the woman's life.
Knox's father told him he had shod that horse and he said it had scars on its hips and flanks, some of them a foot long. Grandfather believed the reason the horse did not smell the panther was because it was up in the tree sometimes and the scent of it went up instead of toward the ground.
The woman was not injured by her fall and made her way back to the house where she had visited and the horse managed to get home. Her husband knew what had happened, got his gun and two dogs, rode to the house where his wife was and got her home safely.

Side Dishes

A place to write new recipes or create your own.

EGGPLANT PARMIGEANA

INGREDIENTS
- 1 large Eggplant
- 1 teaspoon Salt
- ¼ cup Flour
- 2 tablespoons Oleo
- 1 large can Chef-Boy-Ar-Dee Spaghetti with Mushrooms
- ½ lb Mozzarella Cheese
- ¼ cup Parmesan Cheese

DIRECTIONS
- Peel eggplant and cut into thin slices. Sprinkle with salt and place in colander for 2 hours.
- Preheat oven to 300 degrees. Dredge eggplant slices in flour.
- Melt oleo and brown eggplant on both sides.
- In the baking dish place alternate layers of eggplant, spaghetti sauce, mozzarella cheese, and parmesan cheese.
- Bake uncovered for 35 to 30 minutes

FRIED ZUCCHINI CAKES

INGREDIENTS
- 1/3 cup Buttermilk Baking Mix
- ¼ cup Parmesan Cheese
- 1/8 teaspoon Salt
- 1/8 teaspoon Pepper
- 2 Eggs, beaten
- 2 cups Zucchini (about 2 medium)
- 2 tablespoons Oleo

DIRECTIONS
- Peel eggplant and cut into thin slices.
- Sprinkle with salt and place in colander for 2 hours.
- Preheat oven to 300 degrees.
- Dredge eggplant slices in flour.
- Melt oleo and brown eggplant on both sides.
- In the baking dish place alternate layers of eggplant, spaghetti sauce, mozzarella cheese, and parmesan cheese.
- Bake uncovered for 35 to 30 minutes

Notes

HOMEMADE FRIED POTATOES

INGREDIENTS
- Depending on how much you fall in love with these - how many potatoes you use
- 4 to 5 large white or red potatoes (2 people)
- Salt and pepper
- Enough oil to lightly cover bottom of the skillet

DIRECTIONS
- Peel and cut into small strips or squares
- Place potatoes in a HOT skillet (enough oil to lightly cover bottom of the skillet)
- Turn heat down to medium and Cover skillet with lid
- Cook until potatoes are "SOFT"
- Turn heat up and brown.
- Salt and Pepper to taste

GOODY EGGPLANT CASSEROLE

INGREDIENTS
- 1 large eggplant
- Dash of Salt
- 3 Eggs
- 4 tablespoons oleo
- 1 cup milk
- ¼ cup cracker crumbs
- 1 medium Onion
- Chopped ½ cup celery
- 3 cups seasoned dry bread crumbs

DIRECTIONS
- Peel and cube eggplant.
- Boil in salted water until tender (10 to 12 minutes)
- Drain and let cool.
- Beat eggs and milk together until frothy.
- Pour over bread crumbs and blend in onion and celery and add salt to taste
- Let stand until milk is absorbed
- Fold in eggplant and put the mixture in a well-buttered 2 ½ quart casserole dish
- Top with the cracker crumbs and pour butter over the top
- Bake in oven at 325 degrees for 60 minutes and top of casserole is brown

GREEN PARROT SPANISH RICE

INGREDIENTS
- 1 cup Rice
- 1 ½ teaspoon Salt
- 1/3 cup Chicken frying's
- 1 tablespoon Sugar
- ¼ cup chopped Celery
- 1/8 teaspoon Paprika
- ¼ cup chopped Green Pepper
- 1 cup Tomatoes in juice
- ¼ cup Carrots
- 1 pint Chicken Broth
- 1 tablespoon chopped Onion
- 1/8 teaspoon Chili Powder

DIRECTIONS
- Pan fry rice in chicken grease (frying's) until golden brown
- Stir in vegetables and cook for 2 minutes
- Mix in remaining ingredients
- Bring mixture to a boil
- Place lid on pan and turn off fire
- Let stand for 1 hour

BAKED ONIONS

INGREDIENTS
- 3 medium Onions, thinly sliced
- 1-4oz bag Potato Chips
- ½ lb mild Cheese, grated
- 1 can Cream of Mushroom Soup
- ¼ cup Milk
- 1/8 teaspoon Cayenne Pepper

DIRECTIONS
- Alternate layers of onions, crushed potato chips and cheese in buttered casserole dish
- Pour soup and milk over the top of onion mixture and it will cook through
- Sprinkle cayenne pepper over the top
- Bake for 1 hour at 350 degrees

MEXICAN PINTOS

INGREDIENTS
- 2 lbs Pinto Beans
- 2 teaspoons Salt
- 2 large diced Onions
- 4 cloves of Garlic
- Cut ½ teaspoon Pepper
- 1 can Tomatoes
- ½ teaspoon Cumin Seed
- 1 can Taco Sauce 1
- can roasted Green Chilies, chopped

DIRECTIONS
- Soak pintos in cold water overnight
- Drain, wash, and cover with 2 inches of water
- Add salt
- Boil over moderate heat for about 1 hour adding water if needed
- Add remaining ingredients
- Cook over moderate heat for 1 to 1 ½ hours until beans are tender
- For Spicer Beans: add 1 to 2 teaspoons of Chili Powder

POACHED PEACHES

INGREDIENTS
- 1 large can of Peaches
- Brown
- Sugar Cinnamon

DIRECTIONS
- Cook for 10 minutes at slow heat
- *"QUICK APPETIZER OR DESSERT"*

SAVORY BEETS

INGREDIENTS

- 1 can Beets
- ½ cup Sugar
- 3 teaspoons Cornstarch
- ¼ teaspoon Salt
- ¼ teaspoon Cloves
- ¼ cup Water
- ¼ cup Vinegar

DIRECTIONS

- Combine all ingredients except beets.
- Bring to a boil and add beets.
- Cook slowly until heated through

IMPROMPTU SPICED VINEGAR

INGREDIENTS

- 1 quart Vinegar (wine or cider)
- 3 t0 4 Peppercorns
- ½ teaspoon Curry Powder
- 2 teaspoons Dill Seed
- 1 or 2 sliced cloves of Garlic
- 2 tablespoons Fennel Seed
- 2 teaspoons Salt
- 2 tablespoons Anise Seed
- 2 or 3 Cloves
- 2 teaspoons Cumin Seed
- 2 tablespoons Sugar
- 2 teaspoons Celery Seed
- 2 teaspoons Caraway Seed

DIRECTIONS

- Add any or all of these and in addition, anything you find in your spice or herb cabinet if you like.
- Give the vinegar flavor.
- If it is too strong you may dilute it later with more vinegar.
- Bring these ingredients slowly to a boiling point
- Place the vinegar in a closed jar.
- After 2 weeks serve it drained, combined with salad oil in any proportions you like.
- You may add chopped parsley and chopped chives

REFRIGERATOR PICKLES

INGREDIENTS

- 4 cups Sugar
- 4 cups Vinegar
- ½ cup Pickling Salt
- 1 ½ teaspoonful Turmeric
- 1 ½ teaspoonful Celery Seed
- 1 ½ teaspoonful Mustard Seed Cucumbers, peeled and sliced
- 1/8 inch thick 1 thinly sliced Onion for each quart of Cucumbers

DIRECTIONS

- Make and chill a solution of all ingredients except the cucumber and onions.
- When the solution is chilled, place it in a large container suitable for refrigerator storage.
- Slice cucumbers and onions into the solution until the container is filled.
- Refrigerate for five days before using

PEPPER RELISH

INGREDIENTS

- 8 cups Bell Peppers (½ red and ½ green)
- 5 cups Onions, white
- ½ cup hot Pepper (green) Put all through food chopper Mix with: 3 cups Sugar 3 cups Vinegar 2 tablespoons Salt 2 tablespoons Mustard Seed 2 tablespoons Celery Seed

DIRECTIONS

- Put the first three through the food chopper
- Mix with all the remaining ingredients
- Boil 15 to 20 minutes – bottle and seal

PEPPER JELLY

INGREDIENTS
- ¾ cup Green Bell Pepper
- ½ cup Hot Green Pepper
- 6 ½ cups Sugar
- 1 small bottle Certo
- 1 ½ cups Apple Cider Vinegar

DIRECTIONS
- Seed and grind peppers using a fine blade
- Keep out the juice
- Add pepper mixture to sugar and vinegar
- Bring to a rolling boil, stirring with a wooden spoon
- Remove from heat and let cool for 5 minutes
- Add Certo, and let stand until mixture starts to gel, stirring now and then so peppers do not settle to the bottom
- Pour into jelly glasses and seal with melted paraffin

TOMATO RELISH (SMALL RECIPE)

INGREDIENTS
- Large pan ¾ full tomatoes peeled
- 3 or 4 sweet Bell Peppers, chopped
- 3 or 4 Onions, chopped
- 3 cups Sugar
- 1 quart Vinegar
- ½ teaspoon Cinnamon
- ½ teaspoon Cloves
- ½ teaspoon Allspice
- 2 teaspoons Pickling Salt

DIRECTIONS
- Mix all ingredients with tomatoes
- Bring to a boil and then let simmer for 2 hours until mixture becomes thickened, stirring often
- Put in hot jars and seal

TOMATO RELISH

INGREDIENTS
- 2 gallons of Green Tomatoes
- 10 big Onions
- 6 large Green Bell Peppers
- 8 Hot Peppers
- 2 ½ cups Sugar
- 2 cups Vinegar
- 1 teaspoon Mustard Seed
- 1 teaspoon Celery Seed

DIRECTIONS
- Cut tomatoes
- Slice bell peppers
- Cut hot peppers
- Put all ingredients together
- Cook until tomatoes change color
- Put in jars and seal

SNAPPY CHEESE SPREAD

INGREDIENTS
- ½ lb American Cheese
- 1/8 teaspoon Cayenne Pepper
- 1 teaspoon Mustard
- 2 teaspoons Worcestershire Sauce
- ½ teaspoon Salt
- 2 tablespoons Butter
- 1 tablespoon Vinegar

DIRECTIONS
- Allow cheese to stand for several hours
- Cut in small pieces then shred with a fork
- Mix mustard to a past with ½ teaspoon water
- Allow to stand for 10 minutes
- Add the remaining ingredients to the cheese
- Beat until creamy
- Spread on cheese crackers

GREEN TOMATO RELISH

INGREDIENTS

- 6 quarts Green Tomatoes (36 to 40)
- ¾ cup Salt
- 1 ½ quarts chopped Onions
- 3 cups chopped Green Peppers
- 1 ½ cups chopped red Sweet Peppers
- 3 cups Sugar
- 1 ½ quarts Vinegar
- 2 tablespoons whole mixed Pickle Spice

DIRECTIONS

- Chop tomatoes, mix thoroughly, and with salt.
- Let stand overnight, then drain.
- Combine with onions, green and red peppers, sugar, and vinegar.
- Put spices loosely into a bag and place in the tomato mixture
- Bring to a boil.
- Boil gently with spices and cook for 1 ½ hours or until thickened, stirring frequently
- Remove the spice bag.
- Pour relish into hot sterile jars
- Fill jars to top and seal
- Store in a cool dry place

ICICLE PICKLES

INGREDIENTS

- 7 lbs Cucumbers cut in round rings

Make the syrup of:

- 4 lbs Sugar
- 3 quarts Vinegar
- ½ box Pickling Spices

DIRECTIONS

- Soak in enough water to cover with 2 cups lime in the water
- Let stand for 2 hours then wash and soak in ice water for 2 hours
- Heat syrup mixture add cucumbers and cook for 2 hours or until dark green in color when done put in jars and let seal

SQUASH DRESSING

INGREDIENTS

- 2 cups yellow squash
- 1 Onion
- 1 stick Celery
- ½ stick Oleo
- 1 can Cream of Chicken Soup
- 1 pkg Cornbread

DIRECTIONS

- Cook cornbread and crumble
- Combine squash, onions, celery, soup and melted oleo
- Add cornbread and mix well
- Bake at 350 degrees until done (about 30 to 40 minutes)

CORN PUDDING

INGREDIENTS

- 4 ears of fresh corn
- 2 beaten Eggs
- 1 cup Milk
- 1 teaspoon Sugar
- Dash Salt
- 2 tablespoons Butter

DIRECTIONS

- Cut corn from cobs
- Scrape ears
- Combine all ingredients in a buttered 1 ½ quart casserole
- Bake at 350 degrees for 45 minutes or until set

Notes

SQUASH RELISH

- 8 cups diced Squash
- 2 cups diced Onion
- 2 teaspoons Salt
- LET SIT FOR 1 HOUR – DRAIN WELL AND PUT IN PAN
- Mix 1 cup Vinegar
- 1 ½ cups Sugar
- 1 teaspoon Celery Seed
- Add to squash and onion and bring to a boil for 1 minute
- Add: ½ cup chopped Green Peppers
- Let boil for 2 to 3 minutes more then put in jars and seal

SUNSHINE PICKLES

INGREDIENTS & DIRECTIONS

- 2 cups salt
- 10 cups water equal parts white vinegar
- *5% acidity – to cover cucumbers (quantity equals whatever amount in the pot that is entirely covered*
- 1 Grape Leaf
- 2 Peppers per quart
- Garlic to taste
- Dill to taste
- **Put in sunshine for 8 days**

SWEET PICKLES

INGREDIENTS

- 2 quarts cucumbers, sliced
- 2 cups sugar
- 1 teaspoon pickling spice
- 2 tablespoons salt

DIRECTIONS

- Mix all ingredients in a large saucepan
- Cover with vinegar and boil for 5 minutes or until changes color
- Put in quart jars and seal

BREAD AND BUTTER PICKLES

INGREDIENTS

- 4 quarts sliced thin Cucumbers
- 4 medium Onions, sliced thin
- 6 sweet Peppers, cut fine
- 4 tablespoons Salt
- 2 tablespoons Mustard Seed
- 1 tablespoon prepared Mustard
- ½ tablespoon powdered Turmeric
- 3 cups Vinegar 3 cups Sugar

DIRECTIONS

- Mix well Let come to a boil, stirring often
- Put in quart jars and seal

ICICLE PICKLES (SWEET)

INGREDIENTS

- 3 cups lime
- 6 quarts cold water
- 7 lbs cucumbers, sliced
- 2 quarts white vinegar
- 5 lbs sugar
- 2 tablespoons whole spice

DIRECTIONS

- Dissolve lime in water and pour over cucumbers and let stand 24 hours.
- Carefully lift cucumbers out of lime water and wash them several times in cold water.
- Boil white vinegar, pour over cucumbers while still hot, and let stand 24 hours
- Drain off vinegar and add sugar to cucumbers
- Tie spice in cloth and add to cucumbers
- Boil 20 minutes
- Remove spice bag and pack into sterilized jars and seal

SQUASH PICKLES

INGREDIENTS
- 10 cups sliced squash
- 2 cups sliced onion
- 3 bell peppers cut into strips
- Salt down well and let stand for 1 hour. Drain off all juice.

MIX:
- 3 cups Sugar
- 2 cups Vinegar
- 2 tablespoons Mustard Seed
- 2 tablespoons Celery Seed

DIRECTIONS
- Mix together and bring to a rolling boil.
- Put squash, onion, and bell pepper in hot liquid
- Bring back to a boil
- Put in hot jars and seal
- ***NOTE: Mustard Seed and Celery Seed can be left loose in pickles or tied in a cloth when boiling***

HOME STYLE KOSHER DILL PICKLES

- To each quart jar add:
- 1 head of fresh dill
- 2 to 3 cloves of fresh garlic
- 1 small red or green hot Pepper
- Select fresh firm cucumbers.
- Wash and pack in jars
- Bring to a boil 2 quarts water,
- 1 quart Speas Vinegar (cider or distilled) and 1 cup non-iodized salt
- Pour hot solution over cucumbers and seal jars
- Pickles will be ready in 3 to 4 weeks, depending on the size of the cucumbers

GREEN TOMATO MINCEMEAT

INGREDIENTS
- 2 lbs Green Tomatoes
- 1 cup Raisins
- 4 tart Baking Apples, cored
- 2 teaspoons Cinnamon
- 4 Pears, cored
- ½ teaspoon Nutmeg
- 1 Lemon
- ¼ teaspoon Ginger
- ¼ cup Vegetable Oil
- ½ teaspoon Allspice
- ½ cup White Grape Juice
- ¾ cup Light Molasses
- 2 tablespoons Cider Vinegar

DIRECTIONS
- Chop tomatoes, apples, and pears catching any juice that runs out.
- Peel and juice lemon and chop lemon peel.
- In a large pot warm it over medium heat.
- Add tomatoes, apples, pears, lemon peel and juice, grape juice, vinegar and molasses.
- Cook uncovered stirring occasionally until the mixture has a very thick soupy consistency, 30 to 40 minutes.
- Add raisins, cinnamon, nutmeg, ginger and allspice.
- Taste and if necessary add more molasses or vinegar stirring frequently over low heat.
- Reduce until very thick, about 1 hour.
- When finished the mincemeat should hold its shape when stirred with a spoon.
- Cool and freeze in 4-cup portions
- To bake mincemeat pie: take cooked mincemeat and pour into unbaked pie crust.
- Cover with a top crust or crumb crust
- Bake at 375 degrees for 45 to 55 minutes

Notes

SWEET CUMCUMBER PICKLES

- Soak overnight:
   7 lbs sliced cucumbers
  Place in 1 cup of household lime and enough water to cover
- The next morning:
   Wash until water runs clear
- Boil together:
  2 quarts white vinegar
  4 lbs sugar
  4 tablespoons salt
  2 lbs mixed pickling spice
  1 tablespoon whole cloves
   2 sticks cinnamon
  Pour over cucumbers and boil slowly for 2 ½ hours
- Put in jars and seal

FREEZER SLAW

INGREDIENTS

- 1 medium cabbage, shredded for Slaw
- 1 carrot, grated
- 1 green sweet pepper, chopped
- 1 cup vinegar
- ¼ cup water
- 1 teaspoon whole mustard seed
- 1 teaspoon celery seed
- 2 cups sugar

DIRECTIONS

- Mix salt, cabbage, and let stand for 1 hour
- Squeeze excess moisture from cabbage and add carrot and green pepper
- Mix together in a saucepan vinegar, water, mustard seed, celery seed, sugar
- Boil for 1 minute
- Cool to lukewarm and pour over cabbage
- Mix and serve

GUACAMOLE

INGREDIENTS

- 1 large ripe Avocado, peeled, seeded and mashed
- 2 tablespoons Picante Sauce
- 1 teaspoon Lemon Juice
- ¼ teaspoon Salt

DIRECTIONS

- Combine all ingredients ----- mix well

HARVARD BEETS

INGREDIENTS

- 2 ½ cups sliced cooked beets
- ½ cup sugar
- 2 teaspoons cornstarch
- ¼ cup vinegar
- 1 tablespoon butter

DIRECTIONS

- Drain beets, reserving ¼ cup of liquid
- Combine the sugar and cornstarch and stir in the vinegar and beet liquid(reserved).
- Cook, stirring over low heat until the mixture is thickened and smooth.
- Add the beets and the butter and cook until heated through.

Notes

ENGLISH PEA SALAD

INGREDIENTS

- 8 slices Bacon, cooked crisp and crumbled
- 4 hardboiled Eggs, chopped
- 1 cup Celery, chopped
- ½ cup sweet green pepper, chopped
- ½ cup green onion, chopped
- 10 oz frozen (raw) english peas, drained
- 2 cups Miracle Whip
- 2 tablespoons sugar

DIRECTIONS

- Spread all ingredients except Miracle Whip and sugar on lettuce leaves
- Mix Miracle Whip and sugar together and spread over salad on leaves
- Sprinkle with grated cheese

SQUASH DRESSING

INGREDIENTS

- 2 cups Yellow Squash
- 1 Onion
- 1 stick Celery
- ½ stick Oleo
- 1 can Cream of Chicken Soup
- 1 pkg Cornbread

DIRECTIONS

- Cook cornbread and crumble
- Combine squash, onions, celery, soup and melted oleo
- Add cornbread and mix well
- Bake at 350 degrees until done (about 30 to 40 minutes)

"OUR" BREAD AND BUTTER PICKLES

INGREDIENTS

- 4 onions
- 1 sweet pepper
- ¼ cup salt
- 2 ½ cups vinegar
- 2 ½ cups sugar
- 1 tablespoon mustard seed
- ½ teaspoon turmeric
- ¼ teaspoon cloves

DIRECTIONS

- Slice cucumbers as thin as possible
- Chip onion and peppers and add salt
- Let stand 3 hours and then drain
- Heat thoroughly the vinegar, sugar, and spices and add cucumbers
- Heat but do not boil
- Pack in jars while hot

CHEESE ROLL

INGREDIENTS

- ½ lb pkg Old English Cheese
- 1 - 3 oz pkg cream cheese
- ½ cup chopped nuts
- 1 button garlic, grated

DIRECTIONS

- Mix all ingredients until well blended
- Roll into a ball
- Then roll over nuts
- Sprinkle with Paprika if desired
- Refrigerate

Notes

SHOT DIRECTED BY THE BIBLE VERSE

MY grandfather was quite a character. He would have visitors come to see him just to hear his stories. One of those visitors was an editor of The Paris News. He was so entralled by Granddad that he published some of his tails – called Backward Glances. This is one of those stories:

In some parts of the bottom of Sulphur and Sabine River were growths of trees, bushes, brambles, so closely interlaced that it was not possible to ride through them in some places. Such a thicket grew northwest of Greenville a hundred years ago. It was known as Black Cat thicket, because of the harboring animals called cats or panthers, besides deer and other game. Knox, my granddad, would tell him that his father, who was a smith (blacksmith), made the charcoal for his forge from boisd'arc which he burned in a pit in the thicket. One day he went to the ticket to see how the burning was progressing. It needed watching from time to time to prevent it burning too fast. The smith (my great grandfather) took his gun thinking he might kill a deer or a turkey.

GOING A SHORT piece into the thicket he sat on a log, expecting that he would get sight of something to shoot, and he did, though not what he expected. Hearing a a slight rustling of the leaves and breaking of twigs behind him he turned his head and saw a "cat" not more than twenty feet from him. The animal was settled for a jump and knowing it was impossible for him to escape by running Scott kept his eyes on the cat's eyes, turned slowly around on the log and put a bullet between and just above the cat's eyes.

He had heard old hunters say that if a cat was given a death shot after it had set itself for its leap that it would make the leap. Having no choice he made the shot but the cat did not leap. It just settled a little closer to the ground and was dead. The cat measured nine feet from the end of its nose to the end of its tail and was an extra large one. The smith told his son that what nerved him to make the shot was the Bible verse that says that a man shall have dominion over the animals, and he decided to put it into effect.

Main Dishes

A place to write new recipes or create your own.

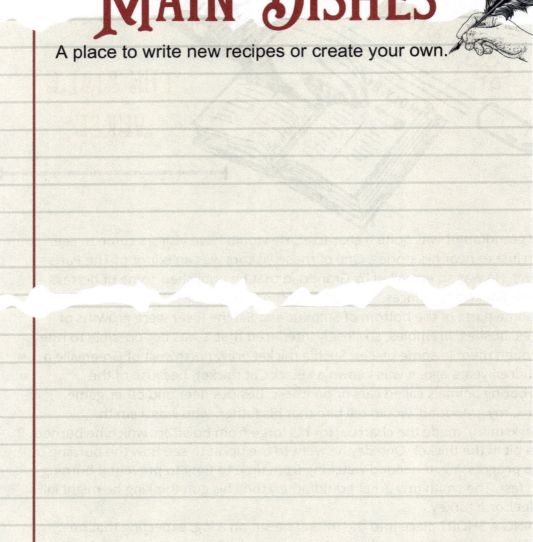

BREAKFAST

HAM AND EGGS – A-LA-SWISS

INGREDIENTS
- 3 English Muffins
- Sliced Boiled Eggs
- Mayonnaise
- Sliced Ham
- Swiss Cheese

DIRECTIONS
- Line muffins with ham, then boiled eggs, Mayonnaise and Swiss Cheese on top
- Place in oven until cheese is melted

HOMEMADE CREAM GRAVY

INGREDIENTS
- 3 to 4 tablespoons oil or drippings from frying hamburger steak
- 2 tablespoons Flour
- Milk
- Salt
- Pepper

DIRECTIONS
- Put oil in skillet (or use drippings)
- Make sure the oil is hot.
- Stir in flour making sure all lumps are out before adding milk
- Add milk slowly, stirring constantly, using as much milk as needed until you get a good thickness (not too thick)
- Add salt and pepper to taste
- Serve over Chicken Fried Steak, Eggs, Biscuits

HOMEMADE FRIED POTATOES

INGREDIENTS
- Depending on how much you fall in love with these - how many potatoes you use
- 4 to 5 large white or red potatoes (2 people)
- Peel and cut into small strips or squares

DIRECTIONS
- Peel and cut into small strips or squares
- Place potatoes in a HOT skillet (enough oil to lightly cover the bottom of the skillet)
- Turn heat down to medium and Cover skillet with lid
- Cook until potatoes are "SOFT"
- Turn the heat up and brown.
- Salt and Pepper to taste

BISCUITS

INGREDIENTS
- 2 cups Flour, sifted
- 1 heaping tablespoon Baking Powder
- 2 tablespoons shortening
- Dash salt
- 1 cup Buttermilk

DIRECTIONS
- Stir and roll on wax paper and cut out with a cookie-cutter
- Bake at 400 degrees for 10 to 12 minutes

Notes

EGG MUFFINS

INGREDIENTS

- 1 cup sugar
- 1 egg
- ¼ cup milk
- Enough flour to mix well

DIRECTIONS

- Put mixture in a muffin tin
- Cook at 350 degrees until done - about 10 minutes

LIGHT WAFFLES

INGREDIENTS

- 2 cups pancake mix
- 2 eggs
- 2 cups milk
- 1/3 cup Crisco (solid)

DIRECTIONS

- Mix all ingredients
- Melt Crisco in a skillet
- Drop by spoonfuls in hot grease
- turn when brown on one side

MILE HIGH BISCUITS

INGREDIENTS

- 2 cups flour
- 2 tablesppons sugar
- 1 1/4 teaspoons baking powder
- 3/4 teaspoon Cream of Tarter
- 3/4 teaspoon salt
- 3/4 cup shortening
- 1 egg, beaten
- 3/4 cup milk

DIRECTIONS

- Peel and cut into small strips or squares
- Place potatoes in a HOT skillet (enough oil to lightly cover the bottom of the skillet)
- Turn heat down to medium and Cover skillet with lid
- Cook until potatoes are "SOFT"
- Turn the heat up and brown.
- Salt and Pepper to taste

BISCUITS

INGREDIENTS

- 2 cups Flour, sifted
- 1 heaping tablespoon Baking Powder
- 2 tablespoons shortening
- Dash salt
- 1 cup Buttermilk

DIRECTIONS

- Stir and roll on wax paper and cut out with a cookie-cutter
- Bake at 400 degrees for 10 to 12 minutes

QUICK STICKY BUNS

INGREDIENTS

- 2 Tablespoons margarine
- ¼ cup firmly packed brown sugar
- ¼ teaspoon ground cinnamon
- ¼ cup Karo light or dark syrup
- ¼ cup chopped nuts
- ¼ cup seedless raisins
- 1 8oz can refrigerated biscuits

DIRECTIONS

- In an 8 or 9-inch layer pan melt margarine in the preheating oven.
- Remove from oven, stir in sugar, cinnamon, Karo, nuts, and raisins.
- Place biscuits on top.
- Bake according to package directions on the biscuits or at 400 degrees for 15 minutes or until biscuits are well browned.
- Let stand 5 minutes, invert on a serving plate, and remove pan

BLUEBERRY MUFFINS

INGREDIENTS

- 1 ½ cups Flour, sifted
- ½ cup Sugar
- 2 teaspoonfuls Baking Powder
- ½ teaspoon Salt
- 1 Egg, beaten
- ½ cup Salad Oil
- ½ cup Milk
- 1 cup fresh or frozen Blueberries (drained)

DIRECTIONS

- Sift the dry ingredients together in a mixing bowl
- Combine the egg, oil, and milk and add to the dry ingredients
- Stir just until the ingredients are blended
- Fold in the blueberries
- Fill greased muffin cups 2/3 full
- Bake in a hot oven 400 degrees for 20 to 25 minutes

PEACHY LEMON BISCUITS

INGREDIENTS

- 1 can Biscuits
- 2 tablespoons powdered Lemonade Mix
- 2 tablespoons Sugar
- 3 tablespoons Oleo
- 10 teaspoons Peach Preserves (or your choice)

DIRECTIONS

- Combine and mix lemonade mix and sugar.
- Dip both sides of the biscuits in melted butter then in the sugar mix
- Arrange in a greased 9-inch pan.
- Make a deep thumbprint in the center of each biscuit.
- Fill the hole with preserves (your choice – does not have to be peach)
- Bake at 375 degrees for 15 to 20 minutes or until brown
- Let stand for 10 minutes before turning onto a serving plate

Beef Dishes

Hamburger Steak

INGREDIENTS

- 1 lb ground Meat
- A small amount of Salt
- A small amount of Pepper
- 2 Onions, chopped and cooked

DIRECTIONS

- Mix together with enough flour to stay together
- Brown both sides then cook slow until done

Chili Pie

INGREDIENTS

- Large can Wolf Brand Chili
- Large can Tamales
- Large package Fritos

DIRECTIONS

- Mix together and cook until hot

Bar-B-Que Spare Ribs

INGREDIENTS

- 4 lbs Spare Ribs
- 1 can Tomato Soup
- 1 Onion
- 2 tablespoons Hot Sauce

DIRECTIONS

- Cut ribs into small pieces.
- Brown ribs well
- Sprinkle finely chopped onions over the ribs
- Mix soup with hot sauce and pour over the ribs
- Cook until done

Meat Loaf

INGREDIENTS

- 1 lb Hamburger
- ½ can Tomato Sauce
- 1 Egg
- ½ cup Water
- 1 medium Onion, chopped
- 1 teaspoon Garlic Powder
- 1 Bell Pepper, chopped
- 12 to 14 saltine crackers, minced (also try Ritz crackers)
- ½ cup Tomato Sauce
- 1 teaspoon Vinegar
- 2 tablespoons Brown Sugar

DIRECTIONS

- Mix hamburger, onions, bell pepper, and garlic powder, tomato sauce, egg, crackers, and water.
- Put in a casserole dish
- ADD: ½ cup Tomato Sauce, Vinegar, Brown Sugar
- Mix together and put on top of the meatloaf
- Cook at 350 degrees for 1 hour

Hamburger Patties

INGREDIENTS

- 1 lb ground Meat
- 1 Egg
- Small amount of Salt
- 1 small sweet Pepper
- 1 Onion, chopped and cooked
- Flour

DIRECTIONS

- Mix together with enough flour to hold patties together
- Cook until done

CHICKEN FRIED STEAK

INGREDIENTS

- 2 lbs hamburger
- Salt
- Pepper
- 2 large eggs
- Flour
- Milk

DIRECTIONS

- Take and make patties out of hamburger meat,
- mixing in eggs to hold the meat together, flattening it out to a thin thickness
- Put milk in a bowl
- Gently dip the flattened hamburger patty in liquid
- Mix salt and pepper in flour
- Take hamburger patty place on flour and cover both sides
- Fry in hot oil turning when brown on 1 side

QUICK HAMBURGER CASSEROLE

INGREDIENTS

- 1 or 2 lbs Hamburger meat
- 1 large Onion, minced
- 1 can Rotel
- 1 can Ranch Style Beans
- 1 pkg Taco Seasoning
- 1 can Whole Kernal Corn
- 1 can Cream of Mushroom Soup
- 1 large package regular Doritos (or any other brand)
- 1 bag shredded cheese

DIRECTIONS

- Cook hamburger meat and onions until done
- Add all other ingredients and stir well
- Spray a 9X12 pan with PAM or coat it with butter to keep it from sticking
- Line pan with ½ bag of the crushed chips
- Pour all mixed ingredients into a pan
- Top with the bag of shredded cheese and the remaining crushed chips
- Bake at 350 degrees for 20 to 30 minutes

Tex-Mex Dishes

Mexican Beef

INGREDIENTS

- 2 lbs boneless round steak
- 1 clove garlic, minced
- ¼ teaspoon pepper
- ½ teaspoon salt
- 2 tablespoons chili powder
- 1-12 oz can tomato paste
- 1 large onion, chopped
- 1 beef bouillon cube, crushed
- 1-16 oz can tomatoes, cut in pieces
- 1 -16 oz can kidney beans, drained

DIRECTIONS

- Spread meat with a mixture of garlic, pepper, salt, chili powder and tomato paste.
- Cut into ½-inch wide strips.
- Place in slow cooker.
- Cover with onion, bouillon cube, and tomatoes
- Cover and cook on low for 6 to 8 hours.
- Turn on High and add beans
- Cook for 30 more minutes.
- Serve on a bed of rice

Taco Soup

INGREDIENTS

- 1 ½ lbs ground meat
- 1 large onion
- 1 can Ranch Style Beans
- 1 can stewed tomatoes
- 1 can Rotel Tomatoes
- 1 can whole kernel corn
- 1 can hominy
- 1 package taco seasoning

DIRECTIONS

- Brown meat and onion until well done
- ADD: Ranch Style Beans, Stewed Tomatoes, Rotel Tomatoes, Corn, Hominy, and Taco Seasoning
- Add enough water to make a good soup and let simmer for about 30 minutes

Chicken Enchiladas

INGREDIENTS

- 4 Chicken breasts (or 1 whole chicken) boiled and de-boned (shredded in small pieces)
- Medium onion, chopped
- 10 corn tortillas (cut in quarters)
- 1 can Rotel Tomatoes
- 1 can Cream of Chicken Soup
- 1-8oz container of sour cream
- 2 tablespoons Margarine
- 10-oz Monterey Jack Cheese
- 10-oz Cheddar Cheese
- 10-oz Mozzarella Cheese

DIRECTIONS

- Mix margarine in a casserole dish
- Mix soups, tomatoes, and sour cream together.
- Layer chicken, tortillas, soups, and cheese 2 times
- Bake at 350 degrees for about 45 minutes to 1 hour

Taco Bean Dip

INGREDIENTS

- 1 can Bean and Bacon Soup
- ½ cup Cheddar Cheese, shredded
- 1 8 oz Sour Cream
- 1 teaspoon dried Minced Onion
- 1 package Taco Seasoning Mix

DIRECTIONS

- Mix everything together except the sour cream.
- Cook over medium heat for 8 minutes.
- Let cool and add sour cream.

CREAM TACOS

INGREDIENTS
- 1 lb Chili
- 2 cans El Rancho Beans
- 1 can Rotel Tomatoes
- 1 lb of Velveeta Cheese
- ½ pint whipping cream (not whipped)
- Fritos or Doritos

DIRECTIONS
- Heat together chili, beans, and tomatoes.
- While hot add 1 lb of Velveeta and whipping cream (not whipped)
- Serve over Fritos or Doritos

TACO SOUP

INGREDIENTS
- 1 lb Beef
- 1 pkg Taco Powder
- 1 can Pinto Beans
- 1 can whole Hominy or Potatoes
- 1 can whole kernel Corn
- 1 can Rotel Tomatoes
- 1 can stewed Tomatoes

DIRECTIONS
- Stir in taco powder and add all canned goods
- Add 2 cans of water
- Cook until hot

CHILI CON CARNE

INGREDIENTS
- 1 lb ground beef
- 1 ¼ cup minced onion
- 2 ½ cups kidney beans
- 1 1/3 cups Condensed Tomato Soup
- 2 tablespoons Chili Powder
- 1 tablespoon flour
- 3 tablespoons water
- 1 teaspoon salt

DIRECTIONS
- Cook beef and onions until browned in butter or drippings.
- Add beans and soup and the rest of the ingredients.
- Continue to cook for 45 minutes over low heat
- Stirring frequently.

TEXAS TWO-STEP CHICKEN PICANTE

INGREDIENTS
- 1 ½ cup Pace Picante Sauce
- 3 tablespoons packed brown sugar
- 1 tablespoon Dijon-style Mustard
- 4 skinless boneless chicken breasts
- 3 cups hot cooked rice

DIRECTIONS
- Mix picante sauce, sugar, and mustard.
- Place chicken in 2-quart shallow baking dish
- Pour mixture over chicken
- Bake at 400 degrees for 30 minutes
- Test chicken to make sure done
- Serve over cooked rice

BRUNCH BURRITOS

Preparing
20 Minutes

Cooking
30 Minutes

Serve
10 Minutes

INGREDIENTS

- 1 large Green Pepper, chopped
- 2/3 cup Onions, chopped
- 2 tablespoons Oleo
- 8 Eggs, slightly beaten
- 1 cup shredded Cheddar Cheese
- 1 ½ cup Picante Sauce
- 8 Flour Tortillas

DIRECTIONS

- Cook green peppers, onions, and oleo in a skillet until tender.
- Combine eggs and cheese in a skillet.
- Cook over medium heat, stirring frequently until eggs set and cheese is melted.
- Heat Picante sauce in a small skillet until warm.
- Dip each tortilla into the sauce.
- Spoon about ½ cup egg mixture onto the center of each tortilla.
- Fold 2 sides over egg mixture
- Place in a 13 X 9-inch baking dish.
- Top with remaining sauce.
- Bake at 350 degrees until hot, for about 10 minutes.
- Top with sour cream if desired.

TAMALES

Preparing 1 Hour **Cooking** 1 Hour **Serve** 10 Minutes

DOUGH: FILLING:

INGREDIENTS

- 5 lbs Masa
- ¾ lb fat Pork meat
- ½ cup Fat
- ¾ lb Veal or Beef
- Meat Stock
- 3 tablespoons Chili Powder
- Salt to taste
- 3 cups hot Water
- 1 clove Garlic, chopped fine
- 1 large Onion chopped fine
- 3 lbs White Corn
- 2 tablespoons Lime
- 3 quarts Water

DIRECTIONS

- Boil both meats.
- When tender, remove meat and drain stock, setting it aside to use on dough
- Cut meat into small cubes or coarse ground.
- Heat 3 tablespoons of lard in a skillet, add meat, and brown

IN THE HOT WATER:

- Mix the chili powder and mix well.
- Add to the meat and mix well.
- Allow to simmer for about ½ hour
- Mix the Masa with salt, fat, and stock
- Beat well with a wooden spoon to make light

TAMALES: CONTINUED

TO PREPARE CORN HUSKS:
Cut or chop off each of the husk, open up and clean well
Put into boiling water for 1 hour
Husks should be about 6 or 7 inches long and 2 ½ inches wide

TO PREPARE MASA:
3 lbs White Corn
2 tablespoons Lime
3 quarts Water
Place corn in kettle, add water and line and allow to boil for about 2 hours, or until corn begins to peel. Remove from fire and cool

Rub corn between the hands until skin and kernel separate. Rinse in cold water until white This is called nixtamal. Run through a Molino grinder or fine food chopper several times. This dough is called Masa. (You can buy Nixa meal in dry form- sometimes labeled Masa, Herrena, or Tamalina

TO PREPARE TAMALES:
Spread a 1/8 inch layer of the prepared masa, about 1 ½ by 4 inches in size, on the upper part of the husk
Put the meat mixture down the center of the husk
Fold over and tie ends with string made from husks or good white string
Steam for 1 hour in kettle

Chicken Dishes

SMOTHERED CHICKEN

INGREDIENTS

- Cut chicken in pieces
- Salt and Pepper
- Four chicken well
- Fry in 1/3 cup fat (oil) until brown
- 1 tablespoon minced onion
- 1 cup water

DIRECTIONS

- Add: Onion and Water
- Put in the baking pan and cook slowly in the oven for about 2 to 3 hours
- Thicken the liquid in the pan with flour by putting some of the liquid off of the chicken in a cup and adding flour.
- Stir until smooth
- Add to the main liquid in the pan to make gravy

STUFFED CHICKEN BREASTS

INGREDIENTS

- ½ cup Spam, finely chopped or ground
- ½ cup 3-minute brand Oats
- 1 can Pineapple (8 ¼ oz)
- ¼ cup seedless Raisins
- 3 tablespoons firmly packed Brown Sugar
- ½ teaspoon Mustard
- 4 whole boned Chicken Breasts
- 4 slices Bacon
- 1 cup Orange Juice

DIRECTIONS

- Combine Spam, oats, pineapple juice, raisins, brown sugar, and mustard.
- Salt each chicken breast and fill it with Spam mixture.
- Wrap each breast with a bacon slice securing it with a toothpick if necessary.
- Place in a shallow baking dish. Combine orange juice and pineapple and pour over stuffed chicken breasts.
- Cover with heavy foil and bake at 300 degrees for 2 ½ hours.
- Remove foil during the last half hour then baste and let brown

CHICKEN DUMPLINGS

INGREDIENTS

- Boil a whole chicken and then remove the meat or open 3 cans of chicken broth
- Take:
- 1 well-beaten egg
- 1 cup sweet Milk
- 1-pint flour
- ½ teaspoon salt
- 2 teaspoons baking powder

DIRECTIONS

- Mix dry ingredients together
- Then add egg and milk
- Drop the batter by spoonfuls into the chicken broth.
- Make sure the broth is boiling.
- Let boil for 15 minutes with batter without stirring.
- **DO NOT COVER**

CHICKEN CREOLE

INGREDIENTS

- 4 Chicken breasts, cut in small squares
- 2 Onions
- 1 teaspoon Basil
- 2 Sweet Peppers
- 1 teaspoon Oregano
- 2 sticks Celery
- 1 hot Pepper
- Box Mushrooms
- Lemon Juice
- Garlic, 2 cloves
- White Wine cooking sauce
- 2 Tomatoes, cubed
- 2 cups Rice

DIRECTIONS

- Brown all ingredients and then add lemon juice and cooking wine.
- Let simmer.
- Fry chicken until tender and add all other ingredients.
- Cook rice.
- Serve all ingredients on rice.

NEAPOLITAN JELLIED CHICKEN SALAD

INGREDIENTS

- 1 5lb Chicken Hen ½ cup Mayonnaise
- 10 hard boiled Eggs 1 jar Pimento
- 1 large stalk Celery 1 small Bell Pepper
- 1 small Onion Juice of 1 Lemon
- 2 tablespoons Gelatin, dissolved in ½ cup cold Water

DIRECTIONS

- Cook hen – separate dark and light meat.
- Grind light meat first with celery and pimento.
- With dark meat grind onions and pepper.
- Fold lemon juice and mayonnaise into each portion of meat, using ½ for each.
- Put dark meat in the bottom of the loaf pan.
- Top with egg yolks which have been run through a slicer.
- Then add light meat and top with egg whites which have been run through a slicer.
- Sprinkle salt on each layer as placed.
- Use 1 cup stock and add to moistened gelatin while hot.
- Press down with a fork to make firm.
- Chill and slice

Fish Dishes

Homemade Fish Dish

INGREDIENTS

- 1 can Salmon
- 1 cup Meal (Corn)
- 1 cup Hominy Grits
- 4 cups boiling Water
- Salt to taste

DIRECTIONS

- To boiling water add corn meal, hominy grits, and salt
- Cook stirring constantly until very thick
- Add salmon and cook until gets very thick again
- Press into a square pan and chill in an icebox
- When ready to serve slice in pieces roll in corn meal and dry as you do fish

Tuna Pasta Salad

INGREDIENTS

- 1 package of small shell Pasta (cooked and drained)
- 1 can Tuna (drained and flaked)
- 1 large Carrot (shredded)
- ¼ cup Onion, chopped
- ¼ cup Mayonnaise
- ¼ cup Milk
- 1 tablespoon Lemon Juice
- 2 teaspoons Mustard
- 1 teaspoon Salt
- 1 teaspoon Dill Weed
- 1/8 teaspoon Pepper

DIRECTIONS

- Combine tuna, carrot, and onion with pasta. Set aside.
- Add all remaining ingredients and whisk until smooth.
- Pour over pasta mixture.
- Cover and refrigerate for 1 to 2 hours.

Tuna Macaroni Bake

INGREDIENTS

- ½ cup evaporated Milk
- ¾ teaspoon Mustard
- 1 tablespoon grated Onion
- ¾ teaspoon Salt
- Add to beaten ingredients:
- 3 cups drained Macaroni
- 1 ½ cups grated Cheese
- 1 cup drained Tuna, broken into pieces

DIRECTIONS

- Turn Oven on to 350 degrees and grease well a 9X13 dish
- Beat well in bowl: eggs, milk, mustard, onion, and salt
- Add to beaten ingredients: Macaroni, Cheese, and Tuna
- Put in a baking dish and cook for 35 to 45 minutes
- Top with ketchup or chili sauce – about ¼ cup

Notes

Seafood Dishes

Manhattan Clam Chowder

INGREDIENTS

- 1 quart shucked Ccams (1 can minced clams can be used)
- 3 cups water
- 2-inch cube of salt pork or 3 slices bacon
- 1 large onion
- 3 tablespoons flour
- 2 cups raw potatoes, cubed
- 3 tablespoons butter
- 3 cups cooked or canned tomatoes
- Salt and pepper

DIRECTIONS

- Wash clams in 3 cups water.
- **SAVE THE HARD PART OF THE CLAM**
- Drain the clams, reserving the water.
- Strain the liquid.
- If using hard-shelled clams, cut the hard part from the soft part.
- Chop finely.
- MIX: a cube of salt pork or bacon with clams
- Saute the pork very slowly.
- Remove and reserve the scraps.
- Add minced onions and the hard part of the clam to the grease.
- Stir and cook this slowly for about 5 minutes.
- Sift the flour over the mixture and stir until blended.
- Stir in reserved liquid.
- Peel and prepare and add: Potatoes, cubed
- Cover and simmer until the potatoes are done.
- Add scraps, clams, and butter.
- Add 3 cups cooked or canned tomatoes.
- Season with salt and pepper.

SHRIMP SALAD

INGREDIENTS
- 2 cans Shrimp or 1 lb
- 1 ½ cups Celery, chopped
- 2 hardboiled Eggs, grated
- 3 tablespoons dill Pickles, chopped
- Toss the above ingredients together
- ½ cup Mayonnaise
- 1 tablespoon Lemon Juice
- 1 tablespoon Ketchup
- ½ teaspoon Worcestershire Sauce
- Dash salt and pepper

DIRECTIONS
- Mix these four ingredients together
- Then add to other mixture
- Serve on lettuce leaves

BAKED SEAFOOD SALAD

INGREDIENTS
- 6 lbs chopped Green Peppers
- 3 lbs chopped Onions
- 1 cup chopped Celery
- 1 cup Mayonnaise
- 1 cup Crab Meat, flaked
- 1 cup Shrimp, pieces
- ½ teaspoon Salt
- ½ teaspoon Pepper
- ½ teaspoon Worcestershire Sauce
- ¾ cup crushed Potato Chips

DIRECTIONS
- Spread in a large greased baking dish. Sprinkle crushed
- chips over the top of mixture and bake in preheated oven at 350
- degrees for 30 minutes.
- May also be baked in individual sea food shells.

Notes

Pork Dishes

Jarvis's Bar-B-Que Sauce

INGREDIENTS

- ½ stick Oleo
- 1 teaspoon Black Pepper
- 1 tablespoon Mustard
- ¼ cup Vinegar

DIRECTIONS

- Mix all ingredients and cook to a boil

Deviled Pork Chops

INGREDIENTS

- 2 tablespoons Shortening
- 6 thick cut Pork Chops
- 1/8 teaspoon Red Pepper
- ½ teaspoon Paprika
- 1 teaspoon Salt
- 1 tablespoon prepared Mustard
- 1 teaspoon Worcestershire Sauce
- 2 tablespoons Ketchup
- 1 tablespoon Lemon Juice
- 1 cup hot Water

DIRECTIONS

- Brown chops in hot shortening. Combine seasoning and
- add water.
- Pour over chops.
- Cook covered over low heat about 30 minutes or until
- tender.

Pork Sausage Enchiladas

INGREDIENTS

- 1 lb Pork Sausage
- Chopped Tomatoes
- ½ cup onion, chopped
- Vegetable Oil
- 1 cup Picante Sauce
- 12 Tortillas
- ¼ teaspoon ground Cumin
- 1 ½ cups shredded chedder cheese

DIRECTIONS

- Cook finely crumbled sausage with onion in skillet.
- Drain well. Stir in ¼ cup picante sauce and cumin.
- Heat oil in a small skillet until hot but not smoking.
- Quickly fry each tortilla in oil to soften, about 5
- seconds on each side.
- Drain on paper towels.
- Spoon about 2 tablespoons of meat mixture on each tortilla.
- Roll and place the seam down in 13 X 9-inch dish.
- Spoon the remaining picante sauce evenly over enchiladas and top with cheese.
- Bake at 350 degrees for 15 minutes or until hot.

SMOTHERED PORK CHOPS

INGREDIENTS

- 4 to 6 Pork Chops
- 2 cans Cream of Mushroom Soup
- 1 large Onion
- Salt
- Pepper

DIRECTIONS

- Brown pork chops with a small amount of olive oil in a skillet
- Take out and place in baking dish
- Slice onion and put on top of pork chops
- Put cans of Cream of Mushroom soup on top of pork chops and onions
- Bake at 350 degrees for 30 to 45 minutes – depending on the thickness of the pork chops

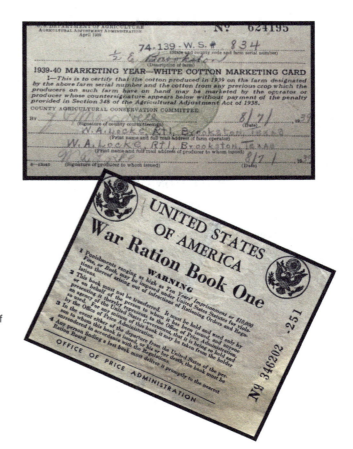

Wild Meat Dishes

Fried Deer Meat

INGREDIENTS
- 3 to 4 lbs Deer Meat
- Flour
- Salt
- Pepper

DIRECTIONS
- Cut deer meat into slices
- Put meat in a bowl of hot water, and shake salt over meat until covered.
- Let stand for at least 1 hour. This will draw out all strong wild taste
- Wash meat off with water
- Put flour in a zip log bag and add meat. Shake until all meat covered with flour
- Put oil in skillet and get hot.
- Place meat in skillet to fry until done – flipping when 1 side is brown
- Remove when both sides are browned and the meat is done, 5 to 10 minutes depending on the thickness of the sliced deer meat

Stir Fry Deer

INGREDIENTS
- 3 to 4 lbs Deer Meat
- 2 large Onions, chopped
- 1 large Bell Pepper, thinly sliced
- 1 box quick Rice
- Olive Oil

DIRECTIONS
- Place deer meat in hot water and shake salt over meat.
- Let stand for about 1 hour.
- Wash off in water
- Cut deer meat up into thin long slices
- Place oil in skillet and add deer meat
- Cook until almost done and add onions and peppers and quick rice
- Add a small amount of water, reduce heat and simmer until onions, peppers, and rice are done

Notes

SMOTHERED SQUIRREL

INGREDIENTS

- 5 to 6 Squirrel
- Salt
- Pepper
- Flour
- Water

DIRECTIONS

- Cut squirrel in portions and place in hot salted
- water to soak out wild taste- about 30 minutes
- Place flour in ziplock bag and put the squirrel in the bag and shake until covered
- Place squirrel portions in a skillet with a small amount of hot oil and brown on both sides. Cover the squirrel with water and turn down heat.
- Cover skillet and cook until squirrel is tender and liquid has thickened to a gravy consistency

Scott's Parakeet Too Little For Tobacco!

That was BIMBO my Granddad's Parakeet. Visitors were fascinated by BIMBO. He would carry on a conversation with you.
This is what he would say:
A preaching parakeet at Cooper admits he's too little to chew tobacco. But, it's a favorite joke to ask his owner, Knox Scott, for a chew! Granddad had taught BIMBO over a 100-word vocabulary.
BIMBO's first words to a visitor are an explanation. He's Clara Scott's boy! Then he'll look out the window, say something about the pretty birds and pipe: " The puppy dog is going to catch the kitty cat." The BIMBO would add: He's a Baptish preachers boy!
BIMBO starts his day with a toast and jelly and joins Knox over a cup of coffee. The rest of the day, he is pretty independent, chattering away to anyone that will listen.
BIMBO usually had an audience.

My Favorite Memories and Recipes

Sunday Memories

Do you remember that 'special smell' on Sunday mornings coming from the kitchen? That smell stays with you for a lifetime because it brings back such wonderful memories of days gone by.

One of my favorite memories is the Sundays Momma would make homemade doughnuts. The smell of the icing being placed on the warm biscuits would take you to the kitchen. While having breakfast I would watch Momma start the preparation for lunch.

MARGIE LOCKE

MARGIE LOCKE SCOTT AND THE LOVE OF HER LIFE MY DADDY, DOUG

Homemade Doughnuts

INGREDIENTS
- 2 cans 10 count biscuits
- 2 cups powder sugar
- 2 tablespoons butter
- Vegetable Oil

DIRECTIONS
- Open biscuits and separate them - cut a hole in the middle of each biscuit
- Put vegetable oil in a skillet and get hot.
- Place biscuits in skillet - takes about 2 to 3 minutes - make sure and turn halfway through cooking to brown on both sides
- Place biscuits on a paper towel to remove the excess oil

Powder Sugar Icing
- Sift powder sugar to remove all lumps - about 2 cups
- Melt 2 tablespoons butter and pour in sugar and stir
- Add enough milk to make a thick smooth icing
- Place on top of warm biscuits
- IF want to make chocolate icing - add a tablespoon cocoa to powder sugar (make sure you sift the cocoa as well to take out any lumps)

BREADS

A place to write new recipes or create your own.

QUICK STICKY BUNS

INGREDIENTS

- 2 Tablespoons margarine
- ¼ cup firmly packed brown sugar
- ¼ teaspoon ground cinnamon
- ¼ cup Karo light or dark syrup
- ¼ cup chopped nuts
- ¼ cup seedless raisins
- 1 8oz can refrigerated biscuits

DIRECTIONS

- In an 8 or 9-inch layer pan melt margarine in the preheating oven.
- Remove from oven, and stir in sugar, cinnamon, Karo, nuts, and raisins. Place biscuits
- on top.
- Bake according to package directions on the biscuits or at 400 degrees for 15 minutes or until biscuits are well browned.
- Let stand for 5 minutes, invert on a serving plate, and remove pan.

SAN ANTONIO CORNBREAD

INGREDIENTS

- 1 cup Flour
- ¾ cup yellow Cornmeal
- 1 ½ teaspoons Baking Powder
- ½ teaspoon Baking Soda
- ½ teaspoon Salt
- 1 cup Buttermilk
- 2 Eggs, slightly beaten
- 6 tablespoons Picante Sauce
- ¼ cup Oleo, melted and cooled
-

DIRECTIONS

- Combine flour, cornmeal, baking powder, and baking soda
- and salt in a large bowl.
- Add Buttermilk, eggs, Picante Sauce, and oleo.
- Stir just until ingredients are blended.
- Pour into a well-greased 8-inch square baking pan.
- Bake at 425 degrees for 25 to 30 minutes or until golden brown

HOMEMADE TORTILLAS

INGREDIENTS

- 2 cups flour
- 1 teaspoon salt
- 1/3 cup olive oil
- ¾ cup water

DIRECTIONS

- Combine flour and salt
- Add olive oil and water
- Mix well
- Divide into 10 balls (golfball size)
- Roll out balls to 4 to 6"
- Turn skillet on and add small amount of olive oil
- Place tortilla in skillet and cook on both sides until golden brown

BISCUITS

INGREDIENTS

- 2 cups Flour, sifted
- 1 heaping tablespoon Baking Powder
- 2 tablespoons shortening
- Dash salt
- 1 cup Buttermilk

DIRECTIONS

- Mix all ingredients
- Stir and roll on wax paper and cut out with cookie cutter
- Bake at 400 degrees for 10 to 12 minute

Notes

CORNY DOGS

INGREDIENTS

- 1 CUP FLOUR
- 1 TEASPOON BAKING POWDER
- 1 TEASPOON SALT
- 1 ½ TABLESPOONS SUGAR
- ¾ CUP CORNMEAL
- 1 EGG
- ¾ CUP MILK
- PACKAGE OF HOT DOGS

DIRECTIONS

- MIX ALL DRY INGREDIENTS THOROUGHLY
- SLOWLY ADD EGG AND MILK UNTIL WELL BLENDED
- DIP WEENIE IN MIX
- DEEP FRY UNTIL GOLDEN BROWN

RANCH STYLE BISCUITS

INGREDIENTS

- 5 cups Flour
- 3 teaspoons Baking Powder
- 1 teaspoon Baking Soda
- ½ teaspoon Salt
- 1/3 cup Sugar
- 2 ½ cups Buttermilk
- ½ cup Oil
- 1 pkg Yeast, dissolved in 2 teaspoons water

DIRECTIONS

- Mix all dry ingredients together.
- Slowly add Buttermilk, oil, and yeast
- Spread out and cut with cookie cutter
- Bake at 350 degrees for 20 minutes

PEACHY LEMON BISCUITS

INGREDIENTS

- 1 can Biscuits
- 2 tablespoons powdered Lemonade Mix
- 2 tablespoons Sugar
- 3 tablespoons Oleo
- 10 teaspoons Peach Preserves (or your choice)

DIRECTIONS

- Combine and mix lemonade mix and sugar.
- Dip both sides of the biscuits in melted butter then in the sugar mix
- Arrange in a greased 9-inch pan.
- Make a deep thumbprint in the center of each biscuit.
- Fill the hole with preserves (your choice – does not have to be peach)
- Bake at 375 degrees for 15 to 20 minutes or until brown
- Let stand for 10 minutes before turning onto a serving plate

GLAZED COCONUT CRESCENTS

INGREDIENTS

- ¼ cup Coconut
- 1 tablespoon Oleo, softened
- ¼ cup chopped Nuts
- 1 can Biscuits
- 1 tablespoon Brown Sugar
- Greased Cookie Sheet
- 2 tablespoons Oleo
- ¼ teaspoon Vanilla

GLAZE:
- ½ cup Powdered Sugar
- 1 to 2 tablespoons hot Water

DIRECTIONS

- Combine 1st four ingredients and blend well.
- Press each biscuit into a 3x6-long triangle
- Sprinkle about 1 tablespoon coconut mixture over each
- triangle
- Roll into a crescent shape and place on a cookie sheet
- Bake at 375 degrees for 12 to 15 minutes

GLAZE:
- In a small saucepan over low heat, cook butter until light golden brown stirring constantly.
- Add remaining glaze ingredients and blend until smooth.
- Spread over rolls

BLUEBERRY MUFFINS

INGREDIENTS

- 1 ½ cups Flour, sifted
- ½ cup Sugar
- 2 teaspoonfuls Baking Powder
- ½ teaspoon Salt
- 1 Egg, beaten
- ½ cup Salad Oil
- ½ cup Milk
- 1 cup fresh or frozen Blueberries (drained)

DIRECTIONS

- Sift the dry ingredients together in a mixing bowl
- Combine the egg, oil, and milk and add to the dry ingredients
- Stir just until the ingredients are blended
- Fold in the blueberries
- Fill greased muffin cups 2/3 full
- Bake in a hot oven 400 degrees for 20 to 25 minutes

MILE HIGH BISCU

INGREDIENTS

- 3 cups flour
- 2 tablespoons sugar
- 1 ½ teaspoons baking powder
- ¾ teaspoon Cream Of Tarter
- ¾ teaspoon salt
- ¾ cup shortening
- 1 egg, beaten
- ¾ cup milk

DIRECTIONS

- Combine 1st 5 ingredients mixing well.
- Cut in shortening with a pastry blender until the mixture resembles a coarse meal.
- Combine egg and milk and add to flour mixture, stirring until dry ingredients are moistened.
- Turn the dough out onto a lightly floured surface
- Knead 8 or 10 times roll dough to 1-inch thickness
- Cut with a 2 ½ inch cutter
- Place biscuits on an ungreased baking sheet and
- Bake at 450 degrees for 15 minutes or until golden brown

ROLLS

INGREDIENTS

- 4 Eggs
- 1 cup Sugar
- 2 teaspoons Salt
- 2 sticks melted Butter
- 2 pkgs dissolved Yeast
- Flour

DIRECTIONS

- In a large bowl beat up eggs, sugar, salt, and butter.
- Add enough flour to make it sticky.
- Add yeast then add enough flour to make a workable dough.
- Grease the top of the dough and set it aside to let rise to double in size
- Make out into rolls and let rise again
- Bake at 425 degrees for 10 minutes
- (Add cinnamon to rolls to make Cinnamon rolls)
- If you do add cinnamon then bake at 375 degrees until done (about 10 to 12 minutes)

DOUGHNUTS

INGREDIENTS
- 1 cup cornmeal
- 1 cup flour
- 4 teaspoons baking powder
- 1 teaspoon salt
- 2 tablespoons sugar
- 1 tablespoon shortening
- 1 cup milk
- 1 egg

DIRECTIONS
- Mix all ingredients.
- Melt shortening in pan in a 400-degree oven
- Pour mixture in pan
- Cook for 10 to 15 minutes or until knife inserted in middle of mixture comes out clean

MEXICAN CORNBREAD

INGREDIENTS
- 1 cup cornmeal
- 1 cup sweet milk
- ¼ teaspoon salt
- 2 eggs, well beaten
- ½ teaspoon baking soda
- 1 can cream-style corn
- ¼ cup bacon drippings
- 1 large onion, chopped
- ½ lb cheese
- 4 jalapeno peppers

DIRECTIONS
- Mix above ingredients and set aside
- Mix these ingredients with 1st set of ingredients
- Mix well bake at 350 degrees for 30 to 35 minutes or until knife stuck in center of dish comes out clean

EGG CORNBREAD

INGREDIENTS
- 1 egg
- 1 cup cornmeal
- ½ cup flour
- 2 teaspoons baking powder
- Buttermilk

DIRECTIONS
- Mix all ingredients together adding enough buttermilk to make a smooth batter
- Put grease (oil) in your pans
- Put in oven to get hot pour batter into greased pans
- Bake at 400 degrees for 10 to 15 minutes

ICE BOX ROLLS

INGREDIENTS
- 2 cups warm water or milk
- 1 pkg dry yeast
- ½ cup sugar
- 1 teaspoon salt
- 1 egg, well beaten
- 6 cups flour, sifted
- 3 tablespoons melted shortening

DIRECTIONS
- Dissolve yeast in water and add sugar, salt, and egg.
- Add ½ of the flour and mix well.
- Add rest of flour and beat well.
- Let rise until double
- Knead down and let rise again
- Knead down and make into rolls
- Let rolls rise until double again
- Bake in a hot oven at 425 degrees until done

My Favorite Memories and Recipes

*Sunday lunch was either at our house or Grandmommy's house.
Our house for those special Sundays consisted of
Pot Roast, Blackeye Peas, Cornbread, and Sheet Cake.*

POT ROAST
Cook in cast iron skillet with Lid

INGREDIENTS

- 1 large chuck roast
- 3 large onions
- Large package carrots
- Large sack potatoes - red or white
- 2 packages of pot roast seasoning
- Small amount of flour
- Small amount of vegetable oil
- 3 to 4 tablespoons flour for gravy (make when roast is done)

DIRECTIONS

- Turn on top burner of the stove
- Place a small amount of vegetable oil in a cast iron skillet and let get hot
- Rub roast - both sides - with flour
- Place in hot oil and brown roast on both sides-make sure you do not burn flour)
- Remove from heat
- Put pot roast seasoning on top of browned roast and rub in. Add salt and pepper
- Place enough water in a skillet to cover the roast
- Cook in oven at 350 degrees for 1 hour
- Peel onions, carrots, potatoes and cut up.
- After the roast has cooked for 1 hour place all ingredients in a skillet with the roast
- Place back in the oven and cook until all ingredients and roast are done - depending on the size of the roast another hour to 1 1/2 hours
- Take all ingredients and roast out of skillet but leave all 'drippings and water'.
- Put 2 tablespoons flour in a glass and mix in enough 'HOT' water to make it smooth - not lumpy
- Turn the burner on top of the stove and place skillet on the burner - get drippings hot
- Slowly add flour mixture to drippings and stir constantly
- Gravy will begin to thicken
- If 1st mixture of flour does not thicken enough -repeat with 1 tablespoon flour mixture (same as above) until you get the 'thickness of gravy' you like.

Sundays at Grandmommy's House

SALMON PATTIES, PINTO BEANS, CORNBREAD, FRIED POTATOES, & RAISIN PIE

GRANDMOMMY, GRANDDADDY AND GRANDKIDS

SALMON PATTIES

INGREDIENTS
- 2 chopped onions
- 2 large eggs
- 1 sleeve crackers - saltines or Ritz- broken up into fine pieces
- 2 to 3 cans Pink Salmon
- 1 cup flour or cornmeal

DIRECTIONS
- Open and take out of can - remove bone and dark skin
- Place in a large bowl
- Add: onions, eggs, 1 sleeve of crackers - saltines or Ritz- broken up into fine pieces
- Mix all together
- 1 cup flour or cornmeal
- Place flour or cornmeal on a flat surface
- Make salmon into patties - about the size of the palm
- Roll in flour or cornmeal (either one is good)
- Place patties in a hot skillet (enough oil to cover the bottom of the skillet)
- Cook on each side for about 3 minutes each side- make sure browned both sides

HOMEMADE FRIED POTATOES

INGREDIENTS
- Depending on how much you fall in love with these - how many potatoes you use
- 4 to 5 large white or red potatoes (2 people)
- Peel and cut into small strips or squares

DIRECTIONS
- Peel and cut into small strips or squares
- Place potatoes in a HOT skillet (enough oil to lightly cover the bottom of the skillet)
- Turn heat down to medium and Cover skillet with lid
- Cook until potatoes are "SOFT"
- Turn the heat up and brown.
- Salt and Pepper to taste

RAISIN PIE

INGREDIENTS
- 1 cup sugar
- 1 stick butter, softened
- 1 tablespoon flour
- 1 teaspoon cinnamon
- 1 egg
- 1 cup raisins (cooked and drained)
- 1 unbaked pie shell

DIRECTIONS
- Mix all ingredients together and pour into an unbaked pie shell.
- Bake at 350 degrees for 40 to 45 minutes or until the mixture is thick.

SAN ANTONIO CORNBREAD

INGREDIENTS
- 1 cup Flour
- ¾ cup yellow Cornmeal
- 1 ½ teaspoons Baking Powder
- ½ teaspoon Baking Soda
- ½ teaspoon Salt
- 1 cup Buttermilk
- 2 Eggs, slightly beaten
- 6 tablespoons Picante Sauce
- ¼ cup Oleo, melted and cooled

DIRECTIONS
- Combine flour, cornmeal, baking powder, and baking soda
- and salt in a large bowl.
- Add Buttermilk, eggs, Picante Sauce, and oleo.
- Stir just until ingredients are blended.
- Pour into a well-greased 8-inch square baking pan.
- Bake at 425 degrees for 25 to 30 minutes or until golden brown

Made in the USA
Coppell, TX
06 January 2024